A Beginners Guide to Fishing

Rods, Reels, and Adventure

By Max Hughes

Introduction

Are you someone who has always been curious about fishing but never knew where to start because you feel overwhelmed by the endless array of fishing equipment and techniques?

And despite all that,

Are you looking to learn responsible fishing practices and become a successful angler?

If so, then this book is for you.

Welcome to "A Beginner's Guide to Fishing: Rods, Reels, and Adventure." In this book, we will provide you with a solid foundation in fishing, teaching you everything you need to know to enjoy and thrive in this great pastime activity.

More precisely, you will learn:

- The essential gear needed for fishing

- Successful fishing techniques

- Catching and handling fish like a pro

- Cooking and cleaning the fish you catch

- How to choose and drive boats, motors, and other fishing accessories

- How to stay safe while fishing

- And so much more!

This book aims to give you the confidence to hit the water and catch your first fish and the knowledge to continue growing as an angler.

Authored by Max, a fishing enthusiast and outdoor writer, this book draws on his years of experience and knowledge in fishing. Max's passion for exploring new fishing spots and trying out new gear and techniques has led him to write for numerous fishing publications, where he enjoys sharing his knowledge and experiences with fellow anglers.

In this book, Max is excited to share his expertise with beginners and help them find the same joy and excitement in fishing that he has discovered.

Whether you're looking to fish in a mountain stream or on the open ocean, this book will provide the knowledge and skills you need to get started.

With Max's guidance, you'll be able to catch fish responsibly and enjoy the great outdoors.

That said, grab your rod and reel, and let's get started on your fishing adventure!

Table of Contents

Introduction _____ 2

SECTION ONE: GETTING STARTED WITH THE BASICS _____ 14

What Is the Importance of Learning the Basics Before Heading Out to Fish? _____ 14

Chapter One: Having the Right Fishing Gear _ 16

Rods and Reels _____ 18

Fishing Accessories _____ 26

Protective Fishing Gear _____ 38

The Right Clothing and Footwear for Fishing ___ 43

Chapter Two: How to Cast a Fishing Line ___ 47

What are the Different Fishing Lines Available? __ 47

The Casting Motion _____ 50

Techniques for Accuracy and Distance when Casting a Fishing Line _____ 53

Tips for Avoiding Common Casting Mistakes ___ 55

Chapter Three: Understanding Baits and Lures ___ 58

The Difference between Live and Artificial Baits ___ 59

How to Choose the Right Bait for Different Fish ___ 60

Different Fishing Lures and Their Purposes ___ 62

Techniques for Using Lures ___ 72

How to Swim Your Lure ___ 75

General Step-By-Step Process on How to Swim Your Lure Successfully When Fishing ___ 78

Chapter Four: Tying Knots – Tips and Illustrations ___ 82

- ☐ What Tools and Materials Do You Need to Tie Knots? ___ 82
- ☐ How to Tie Common Fishing Knots ___ 86
- ☐ Importance of a Secure and Strong Knot ___ 93

Chapter Five: Selecting the Right Fishing Spot ___ 95

Understanding the Habits and Preferences of Different Types of Fish _____ 95

Factors to Consider when Choosing a Fishing Spot 96

Tips for Locating Fish in a New Location _____ 106

SECTION TWO: DIFFERENT TYPES OF FISHING _____ 109

Chapter Six: Fresh Water Fishing _____ 110

Different Types of Fresh Water Fish and How to Catch Them _____ 112

Gear and Equipment for Fresh Water Fishing ____ 121

Techniques for Fresh Water Fishing_____ 122

Chapter Seven: Salt Water Fishing _____ 126

- Different Types of Salt Water Fish and How to Catch Them _____ 127
- Salt Water Fishing Gear _____ 132
- Techniques for Saltwater Fishing _____ 134

Chapter Eight: Fly Fishing _____ 139

1. Different Flies and Lures _____ 140
2. What is the Right Gear and Equipment for Fly Fishing? _____ 146
3. Techniques of Fly Fishing _____ 147
4. List of Fish Caught Through Fly Fishing _____ 149

Chapter Nine: Boat Fishing _____ 151

Gear and Equipment Needed for Boat Fishing _____ 153

Techniques for Boat Fishing _____ 154

Popular Fish Caught Through Boat Fishing _____ 155

Chapter Ten: Surf Fishing _____ 158

Different Types of Fish Caught Through Surf Fishing and Tips on How to Catch Them _____ 159

Gear and Equipment Needed for Surf Fishing _____ 164

Techniques for Surf Fishing _____ 165

Chapter Eleven: Kayak Fishing _____ 169

Different Types of Fish Caught Through Kayak Fishing _____ 170

What Gear and Equipment Do You Need for Kayak Fishing? _____173

Techniques for Kayak Fishing _____174

Chapter Twelve: Bank Fishing _____ 176

The Different Types of Fish Caught Through Bank Fishing _____177

Gear and Equipment for Bank Fishing _____179

Techniques for Bank Fishing _____181

SECTION THREE: TECHNIQUES FOR SUCCESSFUL FISHING_____183

Chapter Thirteen: Understanding Fish Behavior, Anatomy, and Habitats _____184

☐ The Anatomy of Fish _____ 185

☐ Understanding Fish Habitats, Behavior Patterns, and Tendencies _____ 189

Chapter Fourteen: Reading the Water and Finding Fish_____201

How to Identify that There is Fish in an Area____ 202

Chapter Fifteen: Strategies for Fishing in Different Weather Conditions _____ 208

Tips on How to Find and Catch Fish in Different Weather Conditions _____ 209

Chapter Sixteen: When Fish Aren't Biting; What Do You Do? _____ 212

1. Why Fish May Not Be Biting _____ 213

2. The Solutions: How to Change Fishing Techniques and Make Fish Bite _____ 216

3. How to Adjust Baits and Lures to Encourage Fish to Bite _____ 219

SECTION FOUR: CATCHING AND HANDLING FISH _____ 222

Chapter Seventeen: Proper Handling of Fish 223

The Importance of Catching and Handling Fish Properly _____ 223

The Ethics of Fishing: Balancing Enjoyment and Responsibility _____ 225

Chapter Eighteen: Fish Not to Fish — 228

- ☐ Protecting Endangered Species — 228
- ☐ The Impact of Overfishing — 234
- ☐ How to Know the Fish Species to Avoid in Your Area — 237
- ☐ Fish Not to Eat — 239
- ☐ Examples of Fish that Should Not Be Eaten — 242

Chapter Nineteen: Hooking and Landing a Catch — 248

How to set the Hook Properly — 249

How to Play the Fish and Reel it in Like a Pro — 252

How to Land the Fish — 254

Chapter Twenty: Handling Live Fish — 258

- ☐ Tips for Handling Live Fish to Avoid Injuries — 258
- ☐ How to Remove the Hook without Injuring the Fish — 262

How to Release Fish Back into the Water — 265

Chapter 21: Catch and Release vs. Catch and Keep Practices _____ 269

Benefits of Catch-and-Release Fishing _____ 270

Drawbacks of Catch-and-Release Fishing _____ 272

Best Practices for Catch and Keep Fishing _____ 274

The Impact of Catch-and-Keep on the Ecosystem 276

SECTION FIVE: CLEANING, TRANSPORTING, PRESERVING, AND COOKING FISH _____ 278

Chapter 22: Cleaning, Transporting, and Preserving Fish _____ 279

1. How to Clean and Prepare Fish for Transport 279
2. Importance of Keeping Fish Fresh and Clean 288
3. How to Preserve and Store Fish for Future Use 289

Chapter 23: Cooking Fish _____ 293

How to Season and Marinate Fish _____ 293

The Three Main Methods of Cooking Fish _____ 295

Top Fish Recipes You Should Try _____ 305

SECTION SIX: BOATS AND MOTORS _____ 315

The Importance of Having High-Quality Boats and Motors _____ 315

Chapter 24: Types of Boats _____ 318

1. Kayaks_____ 318
2. Canoes_____ 320
3. Jon Boats _____ 322
4. Bass Boats _____ 324
5. Pontoon Boats _____ 326

How to Choose the Right Boat_____ 328

Chapter 25: Boat Safety and Maintenance ___ 331

Tips for Staying Safe when Boat Fishing _____ 331

How to Maintain Your Boat _____ 337

Chapter 26: Motors; Everything You Need to Know_____ 340

☐ Different Types of Motors _____ 340

- ☐ How to Choose the Right Type of Motor for Your Boat and Fishing Style _____ 345
- ☐ How to Maintain Boat Motors _____ 347

Chapter 27: Boat Accessories _____ 350

Different Fishing Accessories and How to Maintain Them _____ 351

How to Choose the Right Accessories for Your Boat and Fishing Style _____ 356

Chapter 28: Etiquette, Licensing, and Regulations for Fishing _____ 358

- ☐ Licensing Requirements for Fishing _____ 358
- ☐ Other Common Regulations for Fishing _____ 362
- ☐ Etiquette on Water and Why It's Important _ 364

Conclusion _____ 367

SECTION ONE: GETTING STARTED WITH THE BASICS

In this section, you will learn the most important things you need to know to at least get started with fishing.

As a beginner in fishing, you may feel excited to jump into the water and start catching fish.

However, fishing is like learning to ride a bike; you wouldn't just hop on a bike and start riding without first learning how to balance and pedal.

But,

What Is the Importance of Learning the Basics Before Heading Out to Fish?

You Will Be Able To Catch More Fish

Learning the basics will help you catch more fish and make your fishing experience more enjoyable.

Imagine casting your line, reeling it in, and not getting a single bite. Frustrating, right?

However,

If you take the time to learn the basics, such as how to properly cast your line, choose the right bait and set the hook, you'll be well on your way to catching fish in no time.

For Safety Purposes

Another important reason to learn the basics is safety.

Fishing involves handling sharp hooks and dealing with live fish, which are likely dangerous if you're not careful. Learning the proper techniques for handling and releasing fish can help prevent injury to you and the fish.

It is Fun!

Lastly, learning the basics is a lot of fun!

How so?

You'll explore various fishing techniques and gear and experiment with different baits and lures. And when you finally catch your first fish, the sense of accomplishment and excitement is truly indescribable.

These are just some importance for learning fishing basics; you can never go wrong with having the basic knowledge or information on any skill or technique.

That said, let's dive right in and learn the basics.

Chapter One: Having the Right Fishing Gear

Did you know having the right gear, bait, and tools can increase the success of your fishing experience?

Picture this: you're standing by the water, rod in hand, and the sun shines down on you. You cast your line and wait patiently for a bite, but nothing happens. You start to wonder if you're doing something wrong, but you're unsure what it could be.

Well, guess what?

Here is where having the right gear, bait, and fishing equipment comes in.

But how?

Having the right fishing gear can improve your fishing success and enjoyment. The right rod and reel combo will help you cast your line further and more accurately and make reeling in that big catch much more effortless. Various types of fish require different gear, so choosing the proper setup for the fishing you plan is essential. Additionally, you must have the right fishing outfit to ensure your safety and comfort.

Before planning a day out fishing, you must invest in the right gear, equipment, accessories, and safety items. This chapter will explore the different things you'll need for a successful fishing excursion.

Rods and Reels

Rods and reels are the first essential things you'll need as part of your fishing gear.

Here are the different types of rods and reels and how to use them:

✓ **Spinning Rods and Reels**

Spinning rods and reels are the most common type of fishing gear, and they are suitable for beginners and experienced anglers alike. The rod has guides that help the line pass through and a spinning reel below the rod.

And where are they used?

These are versatile and are used for various fishing styles, including *freshwater, saltwater, and fly fishing.*

✓ **Baitcasting Rods and Reels**

Baitcasting rods and reels are designed for experienced anglers looking to improve their accuracy and casting distance.

The reel sits on top of the rod, and you must use your thumb to control the spool's rotation.

Here is when to use these tools:

Baitcasting gear is ideal for catching ***large fish*** and is suitable for *freshwater and saltwater fishing.*

✓ Fly Fishing Rods and Reels

Fly fishing rods and reels are used for catching fish using **artificial flies**. The long, flexible rod flicks the line back and forth to cast. The reel stores the line, and you must use your hand to retrieve the line. This type of fishing requires a lot of skill and is ideal when you gain more experience.

Are you wondering what retrieving refers to?

Well,

In fishing, "retrieve" refers to pulling in the fishing line and the attached lure or bait toward the angler. You can do the retrieve at a steady pace or with varying speeds and pauses to mimic the movement of prey and trigger a fish's predatory instincts.

✓ **Surfcasting Rods and Reels**

These rods and reels are designed for beach or surf fishing.

The long and powerful rods allow anglers to cast their bait or lure far into the ocean. The reels are large and can hold a lot of lines, making it easier to ***reel in large fish***.

✓ Spincast Rods and Reels

Spincast rods and reels are a beginner-friendly option that is easy to use. The reel sits on the rod with a button that you must press to release the line.

And what are they best for?

These are ideal for *fishing in freshwater* and are suitable for children and beginners.

✓ **Trolling Rods and Reels**

Trolling rods and reels are designed for fishing from a moving boat.

The reel sits on top of the rod and is used to drag a bait or lure through the water slowly.

Trolling gear is ideal for **catching large fish** since the rods are long and powerful.

✓ **Spinning Reel**

A spinning reel is commonly used for light to medium fishing applications. It is designed to be easy to use and versatile enough for *freshwater, saltwater, and even inshore fishing*.

The spinning reel is mounted on the underside of the fishing rod and is used to cast and retrieve the fishing line. This gear uses a bail mechanism that guides the fishing line onto the spool at the front of the reel. This mechanism allows the angler to cast the fishing line further and more accurately.

Spinning reels are ideal for catching fish like trout, bass, walleye, and panfish.

✓ **Baitcasting Reel**

Baitcasting reels are mounted on the fishing rod and work using a rotating spool as you cast the line. They have a more complex braking system that allows for greater control over the casting process, making them ***ideal for fishing when precision is required***, such as when targeting larger fish species like bass, pike, musky, or saltwater game fish.

Baitcasting reels are often used in ***freshwater and saltwater fishing*** applications.

Obviously,

You don't need fishing rods and reels alone. You must use them with other fishing accessories, so let's look at the fishing accessories you'll need.

Fishing Accessories

Here are the must-have fishing accessories:

1. **Hooks**

Hooks are one of the most important parts of fishing equipment. They are attached to the end of the fishing line and are designed to *catch fish by piercing their mouth or body.*

Hooks come in different sizes and shapes depending on the fish you target. For example, smaller hooks are used for catching small fish, while larger hooks are used for catching bigger fish.

The shape of the hook also varies, with some being more curved than others, which can affect how easily it penetrates the fish's mouth or body.

2. Lines

Fishing lines are string-like materials that **connect the hook to the fishing rod**.

They come in different materials and strengths, with some being made of monofilament, braided, or fluorocarbon materials.

The type of line used depends on the kind of fishing and the size of the fish you want to catch. For example, you will need a more robust and thicker to catch larger fish in saltwater environments, while a thinner line will work best to catch smaller fish in freshwater settings.

3. Weights

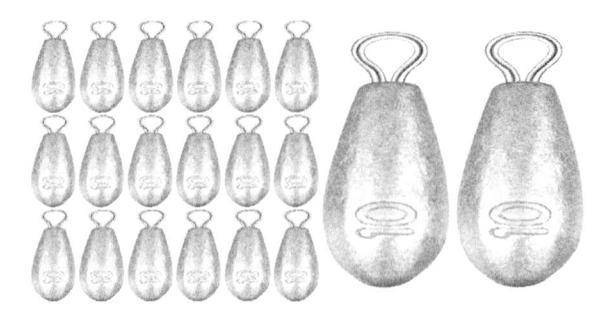

Weights are used to **sink the hook and bait to the desired depth**.

How?

They are attached to the fishing line above the hook and adjustable to suit the depth you want to fish.

They are available in different sizes and shapes depending on the type of fishing and water conditions. For example, you will need a heavier weight when fishing in fast-moving water, while a lighter weight is ideal in calm water.

4. Tackle Boxes

This fishing accessory **_stores and organizes fishing gear_** such as hooks, lines, weights, and lures.

They are available in different sizes and materials, with some having multiple compartments and trays to keep everything organized.

But do you need one?

A tackle box is an essential item for any angler, as it helps keep all the gear in one place and makes it easy to find what you need when you need it.

5. Nets

Nets are an essential fishing tool to **scoop up fish once caught**.

Different sizes and materials are available to suit different fishing needs. For example, smaller nets are suitable for catching smaller fish, while larger ones are better suited for bigger fish.

The material used to make the net can also vary, with some nets made from synthetic materials, while others are from natural materials like cotton or nylon.

6. Rod Holders

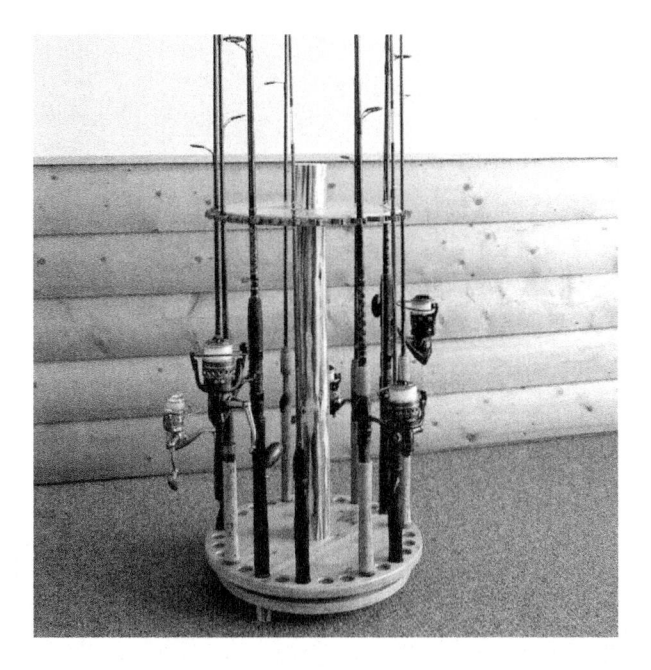

When fishing, it's common to take breaks or switch between fishing poles. Rod holders are handy in such situations as they help **hold the fishing rod when you are not using them.**

They are available in different materials, such as metal or plastic, and designs, including adjustable or fixed versions.

Some rod holders are mounted on boats, while others are attached to the ground.

7. Head Torches

Head torches are valuable *for fishing in low-light conditions*, such as at night or in murky water. They are worn on the head and provide hands-free illumination, essential when fishing in the dark.

Head torches are available in various designs; some come with waterproofing or adjustable brightness features.

8. Pliers

Pliers are versatile fishing tools that *remove hooks from fish and cut fishing lines.* They are handy when handling fish with sharp teeth that can easily injure you.

Pliers are made from materials such as metal or plastic and can have additional features such as a built-in line cutter or a split ring opener.

9. Fish Measurer

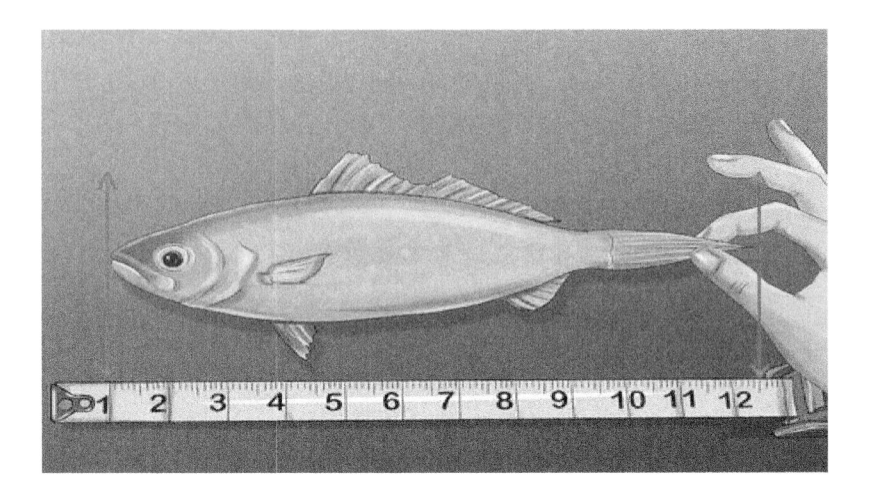

A fish measurer **measures the length of the fish to ensure that it meets the legal requirements for keeping**. This tool is essential for anglers who must follow catch-and-release rules.

They come in various sizes and shapes and are made from metal or plastic. These accessories are also available with features such as rulers or measuring tapes printed on them for convenience.

10. Fishing Leaders

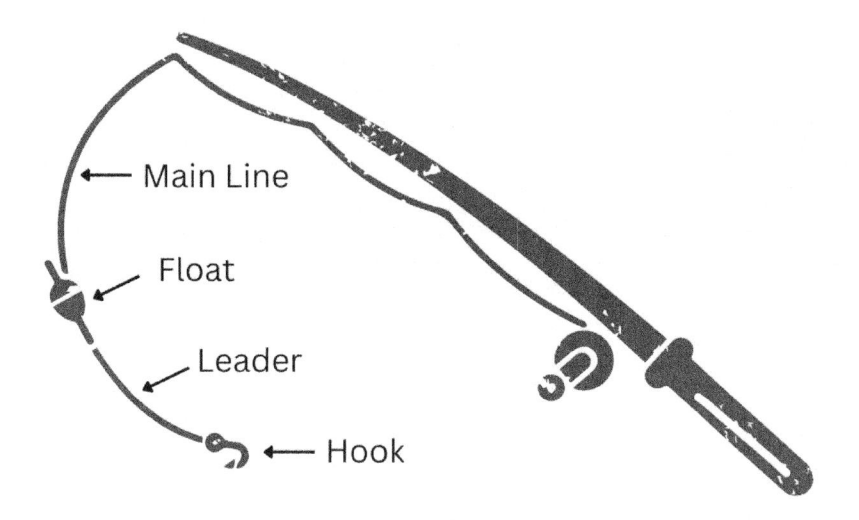

- Main Line
- Float
- Leader
- Hook

Fishing leaders are a piece of fishing equipment that is designed to **connect your main fishing line to your hook or lure**. Leaders are typically made of a heavier, more durable material than the main line, such as monofilament, fluorocarbon, or wire.

Leaders are used for providing additional strength and abrasion resistance, which are likely necessary when targeting larger or stronger fish species or when fishing in areas with sharp rocks, coral, or other hazards.

11. Landing Net

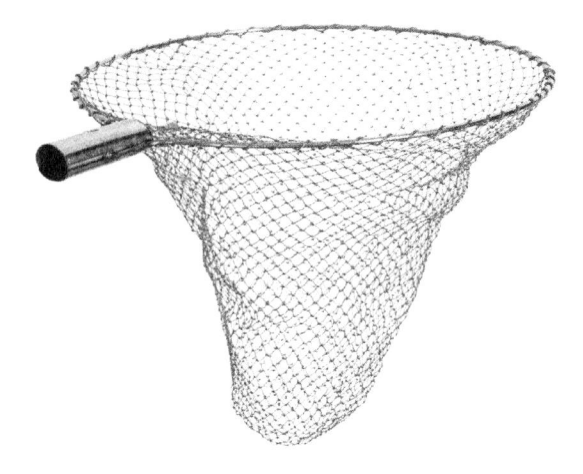

A landing net is an essential tool used in fishing to **_help you land your catch safely and without harming it_**. It's a net attached to a handle and is used to scoop up fish close to the water's surface.

When fishing, you will use a landing net to scoop up the fish once you've got it close enough to the surface. This step is essential because if you try to lift the fish out of the water with your rod or your hands, you risk injuring it, which can cause it to die or be released back into the water with injuries that may make it difficult for it to survive.

12. Fish Finder

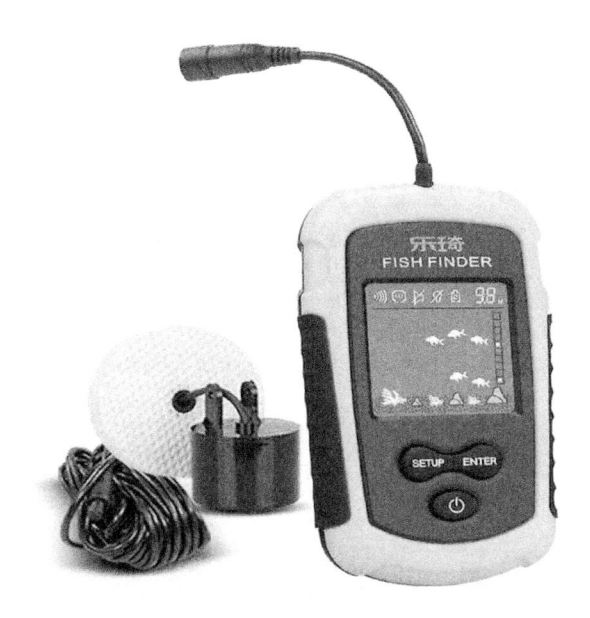

A fish finder is an electronic device that uses sonar technology to *locate fish and underwater structures* in bodies of water such as lakes, rivers, and oceans.

How? You may wonder.

It sends sound waves from a transducer into the water, which bounces back and is interpreted by the device to represent the underwater terrain visually. You can use a fish finder to identify schools of fish, determine the depth of the water, and locate underwater structures such as reefs, drop-offs, and ledges.

Even as you invest in fishing accessories, you must remember that your safety is vital.

Therefore,

Let's look at the protective fishing gear that you'll need.

Protective Fishing Gear

For purposes of safety and comfort, you must have the following items:

1. Sunglasses

Sunglasses are not just a fashionable accessory, but they also play a crucial role in **protecting your eyes from the harmful effects of sunlight**.

Specifically, **polarized sunglasses** are handy for fishing as they can help reduce the glare that reflects off the water's surface, making it easier to see more clearly beneath the surface. This property is beneficial when trying to spot fish or other aquatic life.

2. Fishing Hat

A fishing hat is a versatile accessory that adds style to your outdoor outfit and offers practical benefits for outdoor activities like fishing.

Here are the benefits:

✓ One of the primary functions of a fishing hat is to provide shade for your face and protect your head from the sun's harmful UV rays.

✓ Apart from protecting you from the sun, a fishing hat is designed to keep you cool and comfortable. Its brim shadows your face and neck, reducing the heat that hits your skin.

✓ It also prevents the sun from hitting your eyes, reducing squinting and eye fatigue.

✓ Additionally, fishing hats are designed with ventilation to allow airflow, which helps to regulate your body temperature and prevent overheating.

3. Sunscreen

Sunscreen *protects your skin from harmful UV rays* that can cause skin damage and increase your risk of skin cancer.

Look for a broad-spectrum sunscreen with an SPF of at least 30. Also, remember to reapply every two hours or after swimming or sweating.

4. Insect Repellent

Insect repellent *helps keep bugs at bay and prevents bites* that can cause itching and discomfort.

Choose a repellent with DEET or another active ingredient that is effective against the types of insects in your area.

5. Gloves

Fishing gloves **protect your hands** from cuts, scrapes, and the harsh effects of sun and water.

They also **provide grip when handling fish** and help prevent accidental injury from sharp hooks.

6. Waders

Waders are an essential fishing gear that **comes in handy when you want to get into the water**, like in rivers, streams, or lakes where you don't necessarily fish from a boat or something. They are designed to keep you dry and comfortable while you fish in areas where fishing from the shore or a boat is difficult or impossible.

Waders come in different styles and materials, including chest and hip waders, and are made of various fabrics for added comfort.

Chest waders, as the name suggests, extend from your feet to your chest, providing complete coverage and protection from the water. Hip waders are shorter than chest waders and designed to reach only up to your hips.

7. Life Jacket

A life jacket is an essential safety item you should always wear when fishing on or near the water.

Why?

It **helps keep you afloat if you fall in and can prevent drowning** in the event of an accident.

Choose a life jacket that fits properly and is appropriate for your weight and the type of water you will be fishing in.

8. Buff

A buff is a versatile and multi-functional garment that is used for a variety of purposes when fishing. It is a tube-shaped fabric worn in many different ways, making it a popular accessory for anglers who need protection from the elements.

Which elements?

A buff's primary function is **protecting your face, neck, and head from the sun, wind, and cold**.

The fabric used to make buffs is typically lightweight, breathable, and moisture-wicking, making it perfect for outdoor activities like fishing.

9. Rain Jacket

A rain jacket is essential for *fishing in wet weather*.

But why?

It helps keep you dry and comfortable by repelling rain and preventing moisture from seeping through.

Look for a jacket with breathable fabric and waterproof zippers for added protection.

10.   First Aid Kit

A first aid kit is essential for any fishing trip, whether in a remote wilderness area or a local pond. Fishing involves being out in nature and engaging in physical activity, sometimes resulting in accidents or injuries.

A first aid kit can provide essential medical supplies and tools to help you **treat injuries and prevent further harm** until more advanced medical help arrives.

After investing in the proper safety gear, it is time to choose the right outfits to go fishing.

So,

Let's look at what you should consider when deciding what to wear when fishing.

The Right Clothing and Footwear for Fishing

What kind of clothing and footwear is suitable for fishing?

There is no definite answer to this question, but the clothes and shoes you wear when going fishing should generally have the following characteristics:

1) Breathable

When fishing, you want to wear breathable clothing, allowing air to circulate and preventing overheating.

Therefore,

Choose clothes made from materials like cotton, polyester, or nylon, which are lightweight and breathable.

2) Quick-drying

Quick-drying clothing is a crucial aspect of fishing apparel, enabling you to stay dry and comfortable even when conditions are wet.

Whether wading in a stream, fishing from a boat, or casting from the shore, you will likely encounter water, and when this happens, having quick-drying clothing is advantageous.

3) Sun-protective

When choosing fishing apparel, looking for sun protection clothing is crucial.

Sun-protective clothes typically have built-in UPF (ultraviolet protection factor), a rating system used to measure the effectiveness of a garment's sun protection. UPF ratings range from 15 to 50+, with higher ratings indicating more excellent protection from the sun's UV radiation.

4) Durable

Regarding fishing clothing, durability is a critical factor to consider.

Here is why:

Fishing is likely tough on your clothes because you will be exposed to water and sun. Also, abrasion from fishing equipment is likely to happen. As such, choosing clothes made from durable materials that can withstand the rigors of fishing is essential.

When selecting durable fishing clothing, consider fabrics known for their strength and durability, such as nylon, polyester, or cotton.

5) Loose-fitting

Loose-fitting clothing allows for greater mobility and airflow, making it ideal for fishing.

On the contrary, tight-fitting clothing can restrict movement and become uncomfortable over time.

6) Non-slip

Regarding fishing, proper footwear can significantly improve your safety and comfort.

One of the essential features to look for in fishing footwear is a non-slip sole.

Why?

Having non-slip footwear can help prevent slips and falls, ensuring you can move around confidently and safely while fishing. A non-slip sole is critical because fishing involves walking on slippery surfaces like rocks or boat decks. These surfaces can become tricky when wet, and a slip or fall can lead to injuries or accidents.

7) Waterproof

When it comes to fishing, being prepared for wet conditions is essential, and proper footwear is critical.

So,

Waterproof footwear is **a must-have** when fishing in wet conditions because it can help keep your feet dry and comfortable.

8) Comfortable

Above all, the clothing and footwear you wear when fishing should be comfortable.

Remember,

You'll be spending long hours on the water, so choose clothing and footwear that feel good and allow you to move freely.

Now that you understand what fishing gear you should buy to be a successful angler, let's move to the next chapter and learn how to cast a fishing line.

Chapter Two: How to Cast a Fishing Line

As a beginner in fishing, learning how to cast a fishing line is an essential skill that will immensely enhance your fishing experience.

Sure,

Casting a line may seem daunting initially, but with practice and patience, you can cast like a pro in no time. Whether you're fishing in a lake, river, or ocean, casting a line accurately and effectively is the key to catching fish.

In this chapter, you will learn the basics of casting a fishing line, including the different types of casts and techniques that will help you to become a successful angler.

So, grab your fishing rod, and let's get started.

But,

Before we get started on how to cast a fishing line:

What are the Different Fishing Lines Available?

Fishing lines are available in various types, each with unique characteristics that make them suitable for particular fishing situations.

The following are the main types:

Monofilament Fishing Line

These are the mainly used type of fishing lines. It is a nylon strand that is handlable, stretchable, and used for various fishing techniques.

Monofilament lines come in different strengths, ranging from 2 to 80 pounds. They are suitable for most types of fish, from small panfish to large game fish. Monofilament lines are best suited for fishing in clear water or where fish are easily spooked.

Some commonly used knots with monofilament lines are ***the Palomar knot and the clinch knot.***

Braided Fishing Line

These fishing lines are designed from synthetic fibers strands, such as Spectra or Dyneema, woven together to form a single line.

Here are some of the characteristics of this fishing line:

- ✓ They are solid and have minimal stretch, making them suitable for fishing in deep water or catching large fish.
- ✓ They are also susceptible, allowing you to detect even the slightest bite.

- ✓ They are ideal for fishing in heavy covers, such as weeds or rocky areas, as they can cut through vegetation easily.

The Palomar knot and the double uni knot are the most commonly used with braided lines.

Fluorocarbon Fishing Line

Fluorocarbon lines are made of a single strand of fluorocarbon material that is invisible underwater.

They have a low stretch and are very abrasion-resistant, making them *suitable for fishing in rough terrain.* They are ideal for fishing in clear water, where the fish are easily spooked. Fluorocarbon lines are also super sensitive, allowing anglers to detect the slightest bite

The most commonly used knots with fluorocarbon lines are *the Palomar knots*.

Let's now look at how to cast a fishing line.

The Casting Motion

When casting a fishing line, the casting motion typically involves several steps, which are:

Step 1: Preparing the Rod and Line

You should hold the fishing rod with one hand and use the other hand to hold and release the fishing line.

Before casting, you must ensure the fishing line is straight, and the rod is correctly positioned, as shown in the image above.

- **Step 2: Loading the Rod**

To load the rod, you'll need to lift the tip upwards and backward, which causes the rod to bend and store energy.

Sometimes this motion is referred to as ***"loading the rod."***

Step 3: Executing the Cast

Once the rod is loaded, you should throw the rod forward and release the fishing line.

However,

This motion should be smooth and controlled, with the rod tip moving straight toward the target. As the rod tip moves forward, the energy stored in the rod is transferred to the fishing line, which propels the bait or lures toward the target.

Step 4: Follow Through

After the line is released, you should continue to follow through with the casting motion, allowing the rod to come to a natural stop.

This step helps ensure that the line is released smoothly and accurately.

Overall,

The casting motion in fishing requires coordination between your hands, arms, and body and careful timing and control to achieve an accurate and compelling cast.

Techniques for Accuracy and Distance when Casting a Fishing Line

When it comes to accuracy in casting a fishing line, there are a few techniques you can use to improve your aim.

Here they are:

1) Holding the Rod Properly

Firstly, ensure you are holding the rod properly.

How? You may ask.

Position your hand comfortably on the handle, with your thumb on the rod and index finger below the reel. When you cast, keep your elbow close to your body and use your wrist to flick the rod forward smoothly.

As you release the line, aim for your target and try to land the bait or lure as close as possible.

Remember: Practice makes perfect, so don't be discouraged if you don't hit your target immediately. With time and practice, you'll be able to improve your accuracy and increase your chances of catching fish.

2) Fishing Line Casting Distance

When it comes to distance casting a fishing line, you can use a few techniques to cast further, including the following:

- ✓ Firstly, make sure you have **the right equipment**. A longer rod with a fast action will help you cast further than a shorter, slower rod.

- ✓ Secondly, **use your body to generate power** in your cast. Start with your feet shoulder-width apart, facing your target. Use your non-dominant hand to hold the line and your dominant hand to hold the rod. Pull the rod back and use your body to generate momentum before flicking the rod forward to release the line.

- ✓ Lastly, make sure you are using the right amount of force. Casting too hard or too soft can affect your distance. Experiment with different amounts of energy until you find the best sweet spot.

Tips for Avoiding Common Casting Mistakes

Here are a few tips to help you avoid the most common casting mistakes:

Watch Your Backcast

One of the most common casting mistakes is forgetting to watch your backcast. Before you start your forward cast, ensure your line is stretched fully behind you, and you have enough room to cast on.

Keep an eye on your backcast to ensure the line is straight and untangled before proceeding with your forward cast.

Keep Your Wrist Stiff

Another common casting mistake is using too much wrist in your cast, which can cause the line to whip back and forth, making it difficult to control.

Instead, keep your wrist stiff and use your forearm and shoulder to generate the casting motion. This tip will help you maintain control and accuracy in your cast.

Use the Right Amount of Force

Overcasting or under-casting is another common mistake that can affect the distance and accuracy of your cast.

So what should you do?

Use the proper force based on the weight of your lure or bait and the length of your line. Start with moderate force and adjust accordingly to find the sweet spot.

Practice Your Timing

Timing is everything when it comes to casting.

And,

One of the most common mistakes is starting your forward cast too early or too late. And to avoid this, practice timing by beginning your forward cast when the line straightens behind you. Doing this will help you maintain a smooth, consistent cast.

Keep Your Eye on the Target

Lastly, keeping your eye on the target when casting is essential.

Many anglers look down at their rod or line instead of keeping their eye on the target. However, this can affect the accuracy of your cast and make it challenging to land your lure or bait where you want it.

Instead,

Keep your eye on the target when casting and follow through till your bait or lure hits the water.

Knowing how to cast your fishing line accurately will improve your chances of catching fish quickly and effortlessly.

Let's move on to the next chapter and learn about baits and lures.

Chapter Three: Understanding Baits and Lures

As a beginner in fishing, you may have heard the terms baits and lures but might not exactly know what they are.

Well,

Bait refers to any food or substance that attracts fish to your hook. It could be live bait such as worms, minnows, or insects, or artificial bait such as plastic worms or grubs. On the other hand, **lures are** artificial objects designed to mimic the look and movement of prey to trick fish into biting. They come in many shapes and sizes and are often brightly colored or have added features like hooks, feathers, or beads.

That said, did you know that the type of bait or lure you use could be the difference between a successful day of fishing and coming up empty-handed?

Well,

Various fish species prefer different bait, so choosing the right bait for your target type is essential.

The Difference between Live and Artificial Baits

Live bait refers to using actual live organisms such as worms, crickets, or minnows as bait when fishing. These baits are often used to mimic the natural food sources of fish and are particularly effective in enticing fish to bite.

Artificial bait, on the other hand, refers to synthetic lures and bait designed to imitate the appearance and movement of live prey. These baits can come in various shapes, colors, and sizes and are made from plastic, rubber, or feathers.

Here are the main differences between live and artificial baits:

- One key difference between live and artificial baits is that live bait is often more effective in catching fish that are particularly picky or selective in their feeding habits. This is because live bait more closely resembles the natural prey of these fish and is likely more enticing to them.

- However, artificial bait is ***more versatile*** because it is used in a broader range of fishing conditions and is likely more easily transported and stored. Additionally, some artificial baits are designed to produce specific actions or movements that are particularly effective in attracting certain types of fish.

How to Choose the Right Bait for Different Fish

Choosing the right bait for the fish you want to catch can make a big difference in your success as an angler.

Here are some steps to help you choose the right bait:

1) Identify the Species of Fish You want to Catch

Knowing the specific species of fish you want to catch will help you choose the right bait. Various types of fish have different feeding habits and preferences for certain types of bait.

Here are a few examples of baits and the different fish species they work best on:

- Worms - Trout, Bluegill, Catfish, Bass
- Crickets - Bluegill, Bass
- Minnows - Trout, Bass, Crappie, Walleye, Northern Pike
- Shrimp - Redfish, Trout, Flounder
- Power Bait - Trout
- Nightcrawlers - Bass, Bluegill, Catfish
- Dough Balls - Carp
- Chicken Liver - Catfish

- ✓ Cut Bait - Catfish, Striped Bass
- ✓ Squid - Striped Bass, Fluke, Tautog
- ✓ Waxworms - Bluegill, Trout
- ✓ Corn - Carp, Catfish
- ✓ Jigs - Crappie, Bass, Walleye, Northern Pike
- ✓ Spinnerbaits - Bass, Pike, Musky
- ✓ Topwater lures - Bass, Pike, Musky

2) Research the Feeding Habits of the Fish

Learn about the feeding habits of the fish you want to catch.

Some fish like Barracuda, Pike, Muskie, Trout, Salmon, Tuna, Swordfish, Marlin, Walleye, and Catfish are **predators that prefer live prey**. On the other hand, some fish like Catfish, Carp, Tilapia, Grouper, Snapper, Perch, Eel, Mullet, Bullhead, and Gar are **scavengers that will eat almost anything**.

3) Consider the Water Conditions

Water temperature, depth, and clarity can all affect the behavior of fish and their preferences for certain types of bait.

For example, tropical fish such as angelfish, clownfish, and Betta may be more active and aggressive in warmer water and more likely to strike at a fast-moving lure.

4) Choose the Right Type of Bait

Based on your research and the water conditions, choose the right type of bait.

Live bait, like insects, minnows, worms, and insects, are likely efficacious for many fish species. Artificial lures, like spinners, jigs, and crankbaits, can also be practical because you can get those tailored to mimic the natural prey of your target fish.

5) Experiment

Even if you have researched, it may take some experimentation to find the right bait to entice the fish to bite. Be willing to try different types of bait and adjust your technique until you find what works best.

Different Fishing Lures and Their Purposes

Fishing lures are manufactured baits designed to allure fish and entice them to bite the hook. Various fishing lures are designed to target specific fish species and fishing techniques.

Here is an overview of the main fishing lures and their purposes:

- **Jigs**

These lures are versatile and are used for saltwater and freshwater fishing. They have a tungsten or lead head and a soft plastic or feather tail. Jigs are great for fishing in **deep water**, as you can jig them up and down to attract fish.

These lures are perfect for fishing Crappies, Bass, Walleye, and Northern Pike.

- **Spinner Baits**

Spinner baits are lures with a wire frame consisting of one or more spinning blades and a rubber or silicone skirt. They are designed to imitate small fish or baitfish and are great for fishing in *murky or stained water*.

This type of bait is excellent for catching Pike, Musky, and Bass.

- **Crank Baits**

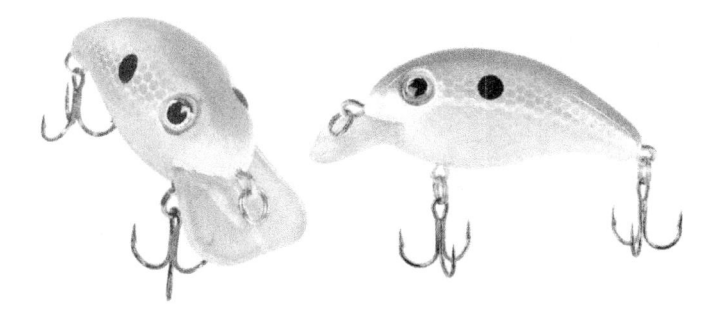

Crank-baits are hard-bodied lures that mimic the swimming action of baitfish. They are available in various sizes, shapes, and diving depths and are often used for bass fishing in *shallow and deep water*.

These baits catch Bass (Largemouth, Smallmouth, Spotted), Pike, Musky, Trout, Walleye, and Crappie.

- **Topwater Lures**

These lures are made to float on the water's surface and imitate insects, frogs, or other surface prey. They are great for fishing in *shallow water or around weed beds*.

These lures are perfect for catching Northern pike, Bass, Tarpon, and Musky.

- **Swimbaits**

Swimbaits are soft plastic lures that imitate the swimming action of baitfish. They are mostly rigged with a weighted hook or used with a jig head and are great ***for catching larger fish*** such as musky, pike, and bass.

- **Jerkbaits**

Jerkbaits are hard-bodied lures that are designed to mimic injured baitfish. They are typically used with a stop-and-go retrieve and are likely very effective for catching **bass, pike, and musky**.

- **Spoon Lures**

Spoon lures are metal lures that imitate the flash and movement of baitfish. They are typically used for trolling or casting and are very effective for catching **salmon, trout, and other game fish.**

- **Blade Bait**

Blade baits are metal lures designed to mimic the movement of a wounded baitfish. They typically consist of a thin, flat metal body with a small blade attached to the front that vibrates as the lure is retrieved through the water.

To use a blade bait, cast it out and allow it to sink to the desired depth before retrieving it with a steady, rhythmic retrieve. The blade's vibration creates a realistic swimming action that can attract various predatory fish species.

Blade baits are versatile lures that catch various fish species, including bass, walleye, trout, and pike.

- **Soft Plastic Lures**

These fishing lures are made from soft, pliable materials such as silicone, rubber, or PVC. They are designed to mimic the look and movement of natural baitfish or other prey and are molded into various colors and shapes to imitate different types of fish.

Soft plastic lures effectively catch many fish species, including bass, trout, walleye, and panfish. They are beneficial, especially when targeting *fish that feed on smaller baitfish* or other small prey items.

Techniques for Using Lures

Having the right bait and lures is excellent, but it is pointless when you do not know how to use them.

So,

Here are a few techniques you can apply with lures to make your fishing adventure more successful and enjoyable:

1. **Vary Your Retrieve Speed**

Fish are often attracted to the lure's movement, and changing up the speed of your retrieve can help entice more strikes.

For example, try a fast retrieve with a crankbait to imitate a fleeing baitfish or a slow, twitchy retrieve with a soft plastic worm to simulate a dying prey.

2. **Experiment with Different Colors**

Fish are attracted to different colors depending on the species and the environment. **Bright colors** like chartreuse are likely effective in **murky water**, while more **natural colors** like brown or green may be better in **clear water**.

Experiment with different colors to see what works best for your target fish.

3. Use a Scent Attractant

Scent attractants can help mask human odors and attract fish to your lure.

For example, using a shrimp scent on soft plastic bait can mimic the smell of real shrimp and attract species like redfish and snook.

4. Try Different Types of Lures

Different types of lures are likely effective for various species and situations.

For example, a topwater lure like a popper or frog is likely effective for bass in shallow waters, while a jig or swimbait can work well for walleye in deeper waters.

5. Match the Hatch

Matching the hatch refers to using a lure that mimics the size, shape, and color of the prey that the fish are feeding on.

For example, using a small silver spoon can mimic the appearance of small minnows that bass may be feeding on. (As demonstrated by the image above).

Now that you know the different types of lures, let's look at how you swim them.

How to Swim Your Lure

First, you must understand that different lures require different swimming techniques.

Here is an explanation of how to swim different lures:

- **Crankbaits**

When retrieved, these lures have a diving lip that causes them to dive and swim wobbly.

To use them, cast out and retrieve steadily, occasionally pausing to let the lure dive deeper or rise closer to the surface. Vary your retrieve speed and depth until you find what works best.

- **Spinnerbaits**

These lures have a spinner blade that rotates around a wire arm when retrieved, creating flash and vibration.

To use them, cast out and retrieve them at a steady pace, varying your speed and pausing occasionally. You can also add a twitch or jerk to the rod tip to make the blade flutter or change direction.

- **Jigs**

These lures have a weighted head and a skirt or soft plastic trailer.

To use them, cast out and let the jig sink to the bottom, then hop it along the bottom by lifting and dropping the rod tip. You can also swim the jig through the water column by reeling steadily and adding occasional twitches or pauses.

- **Topwater Lures**

When retrieved, these lures float on the surface, creating a commotion, often imitating a wounded or fleeing baitfish.

To swim them, cast them out, and retrieve them using various techniques such as popping, walking the dog, or buzzing.

- **Soft Plastics**

These lures are made of soft, flexible material that mimics the look and feel of live baitfish, worms, or insects.

To swim soft plastic lures, cast out and retrieve them using various techniques such as hopping, dragging, or swimming. Vary your retrieve speed and depth until you find what works best.

- **Jerkbaits**

These lures are designed to imitate the erratic movement of injured baitfish and are typically long and slender with a diving lip.

To swim them, cast them out and retrieve them with sharp, erratic jerks of the rod tip, then pause and let the lure suspend in the water column. Vary your retrieve speed and depth until you find what works best.

- **Blade Baits**

These lures have a thin, metal blade that rapidly vibrates when retrieved, imitating the movement of a fleeing baitfish.

And how do you swim them?

Cast them out and retrieve them steadily, varying speed and adding occasional pauses or jerks. Blade baits are especially effective in **colder water temperatures**.

These are just a few lures; there are many of them available, which we cannot possibly discuss in this guide. However, below, we well learn the general process of swimming any lure.

General Step-By-Step Process on How to Swim Your Lure Successfully When Fishing

- **Step 1: Determine the Type of Lure You're Using**

Various types of lures require different swimming techniques, as shown in the section above.

- **Step 2: Cast Your Lure**

Cast your lure out to your desired location. Make sure you cast far enough to reach the fish you're targeting.

- **Step 3: Retrieve Your Lure**

"Retrieve your lure" means to bring your fishing bait or lure back towards you through the water by reeling in the fishing line.

How you retrieve the lure should vary depending on the behavior of the fish you are trying to catch. This motion is because retrieving your lure aims to mimic the movement of natural prey in the water and entice fish to bite.

That said, here are some standard techniques for retrieving a lure:

- ✓ **Steady Retrieve:** This is the most basic and straightforward technique. You reel in the lure at a consistent speed. This technique works well for many types of lures and is likely effective for attracting *fish that are actively feeding*.

- ✓ **Stop-and-Go Retrieve:** This technique involves reeling in the lure, then pausing for a few seconds before continuing the retrieve. This tactic can mimic injured prey's movement and be particularly effective for lures that imitate baitfish or other small prey.

- ✓ **Jerk Retrieve:** With this technique, you use short, quick jerks of the rod tip to make the lure dart and twitch through the water. This technique is likely very effective for *lures that imitate insects, shrimp, or other small prey* that move quickly through the water.

- ✓ **Slow Retrieve:** A slow retrieve involves reeling in the lure at a plodding pace, with occasional pauses. This method is particularly effective for *lures that imitate slow-moving prey* like worms or leeches.

- **Step 4: Vary Your Retrieve Speed**

Fish are often attracted to lures that appear to be moving naturally.

To achieve this, vary your retrieve speed occasionally. For example, you can retrieve your lure quickly for a few seconds, then slow it down for a few more seconds.

- **Step 5: Add in Twitches or Pauses**

Adding twitches or pauses can make it look more natural, depending on the lure you're using. For example, with a crankbait, you can pause briefly after a few cranks, then twitch the lure to make it look like a wounded fish.

- **Step 6: Pay Attention to Your Lure**

Keep an eye on your lure at all times. Watch for any movement or jerks that might indicate a bite. Also, pay attention to the depth of your lure and adjust your retrieve accordingly.

- **Step 7: Be Patient**

Fishing requires patience, so don't get discouraged if you don't catch anything immediately. Try different techniques and adjust your retrieve until you find what works best.

By following these steps, you can swim your lure successfully and attract more fish to your line.

Let's move on to the next chapter and learn how to tie knots when fishing.

Chapter Four: Tying Knots –Tips and Illustrations

Knots used to tie the fishing line to the hook, lure, or swivel are essential in fishing.

Why?

- ✓ These knots are necessary to secure the bait or lure to the line and ensure it doesn't come loose during casting or retrieval.

- ✓ Knots also help transfer the energy of your cast from the rod to the lure or bait, allowing you to cast further and more accurately.

Knots are tied whenever a line needs to be attached to something else, such as a hook, swivel, or lure.

- **What Tools and Materials Do You Need to Tie Knots?**

1. Fishing Line

The fishing line is the primary material used for tying knots in fishing.

The type and strength of this tool depend on the kind of fishing and the fish size you are targeting. For example, you could settle for a heavy-duty braided line when fishing for large game fish like marlin or tuna, while a lighter monofilament line will likely serve you best when catching smaller fish like trout or bass.

2. Hooks, Lures, and Swivels

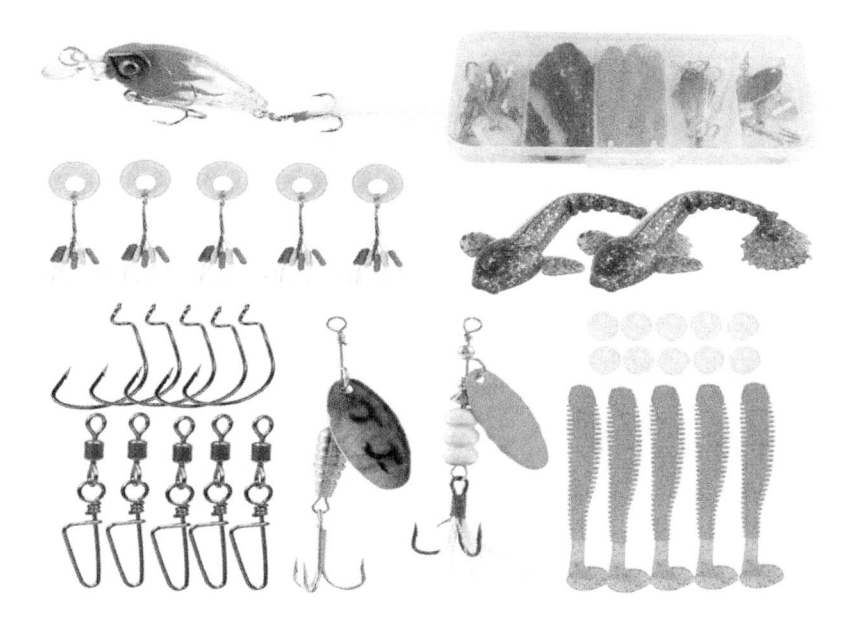

These are the objects that the line needs to be tied to.

3. Scissors or Line Cutters

A good pair of scissors or line cutters are essential for cutting the fishing line and trimming excess lines from knots.

They should be sharp enough to cut through the line cleanly and efficiently.

4. Pliers or Hemostats

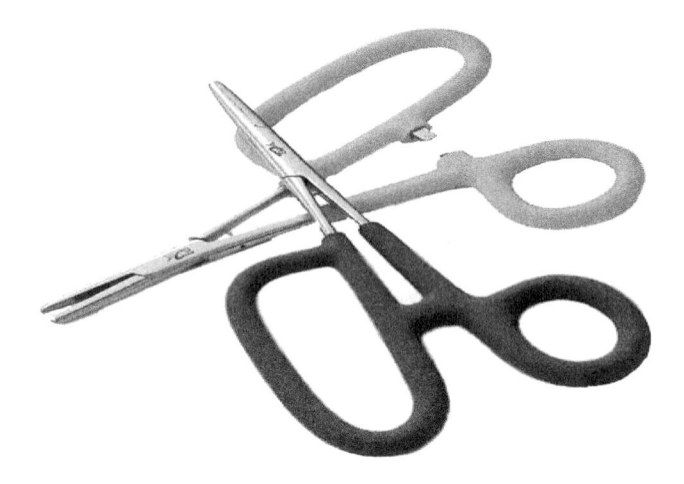

Pliers or hemostats hold the hook or lure in place while tying the knot.

5. Knot Tying Tool

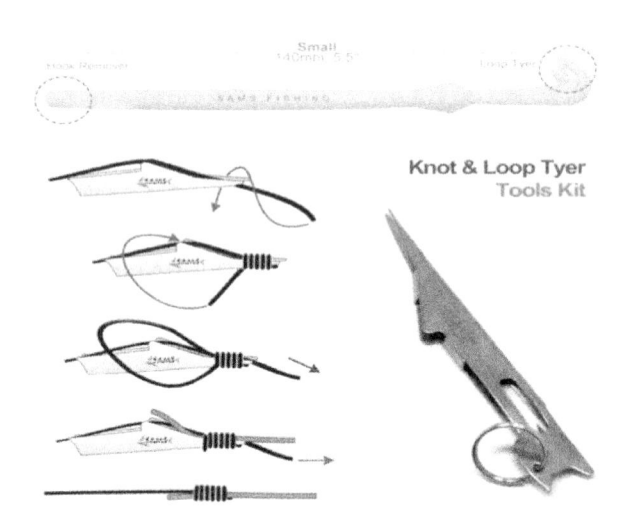

A knot-tying tool is a handy gadget designed to make it easier and quicker to tie knots in a fishing line.

To use a knot-tying tool, you will typically thread the end of the fishing line through a small slot in the device, then wrap the line around the device a certain number of times. You will then use the tool to guide the tag end of the line through the loops created, ultimately creating a secure knot that you can use to attach hooks, lures, or other terminal tackle to the fishing line.

Knot-tying tools are handy if you have difficulty tying knots by hand or when you need to tie knots quickly and efficiently while on the water.

6. Knot Lubricant

When it comes to fishing, knot lubricants are essential to make the knots stronger and easier to tie.

There are several types of knot lubricants available in the market. One of the most common types is *silicone-based lubricants* that are easy to apply and dry quickly. They are also waterproof and can prevent rust and corrosion. Another type is *wax-based lubricants* which work well in cold weather and can help prevent line abrasion. They are also easy to apply and provide a smooth surface for knots to slide through.

The most preferred type is ***oil-based lubricants***, which can penetrate deep into the line's fibers and provide long-lasting lubrication.

- ## How to Tie Common Fishing Knots

1. Clinch Knot

This knot ties fishing lines to hooks, lures, and swivels. It is one of the most commonly used knots in fishing.

So, how do you tie the clinch knot?

Step-By-Step Process:

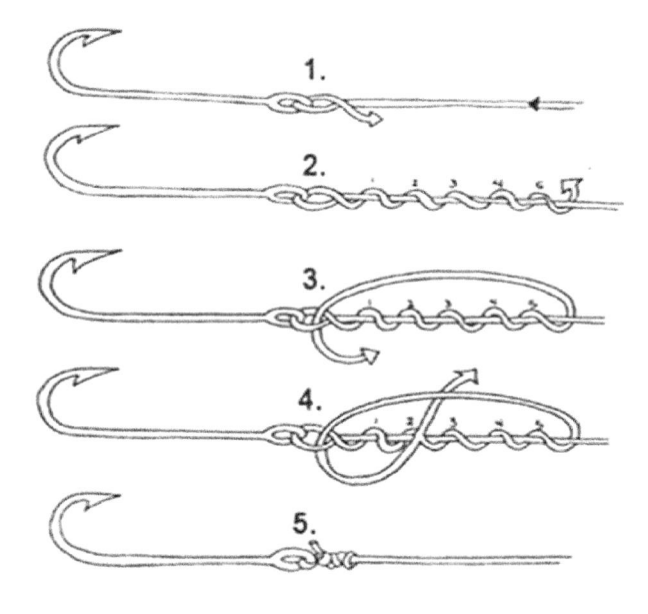

✓ Thread the fishing line through the eye of the hook or lure.

- ✓ Make five to seven turns around the standing line (the part of the line that is not being used to tie the knot).

- ✓ Thread the tag end (the free end of the line) through the loop closest to the eye of the hook or lure.

- ✓ Bring the tag end back through the loop you created, but this time pass it through the larger loop. Wet the knot with water or saliva, then pull the tag end and standing line in opposite directions to tighten the knot.

- ✓ Trim the tag end close to the knot.

2. Palomar Knot

This knot ties the fishing line to hooks, lures, and swivels. It is known for its strength and is particularly useful when using braided lines.

Step-By-Step Process:

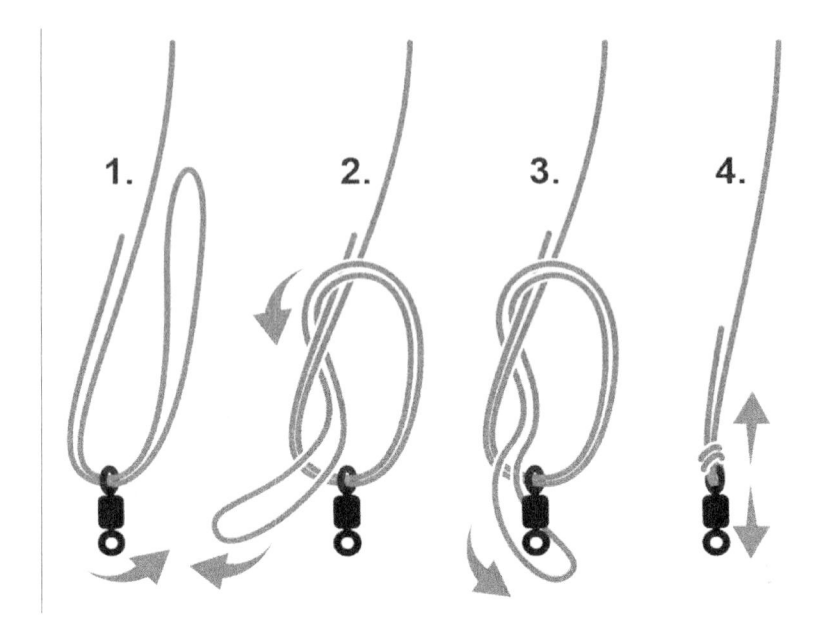

- ✓ Double the fishing line and pass it through the eye of the hook or lure.

- ✓ Tie a simple overhand knot with the doubled line, but don't tighten it yet.

- ✓ Pass the loop over the hook or lure. Wet the knot with water or saliva, then pull the tag end and standing line in opposite directions to tighten the knot.

- ✓ Trim the tag end close to the knot.

3. Uni Knot

This knot ties fishing lines to hooks, lures, and swivels. It is also helpful in joining two pieces of fishing line together.

Step-By-Step Process:

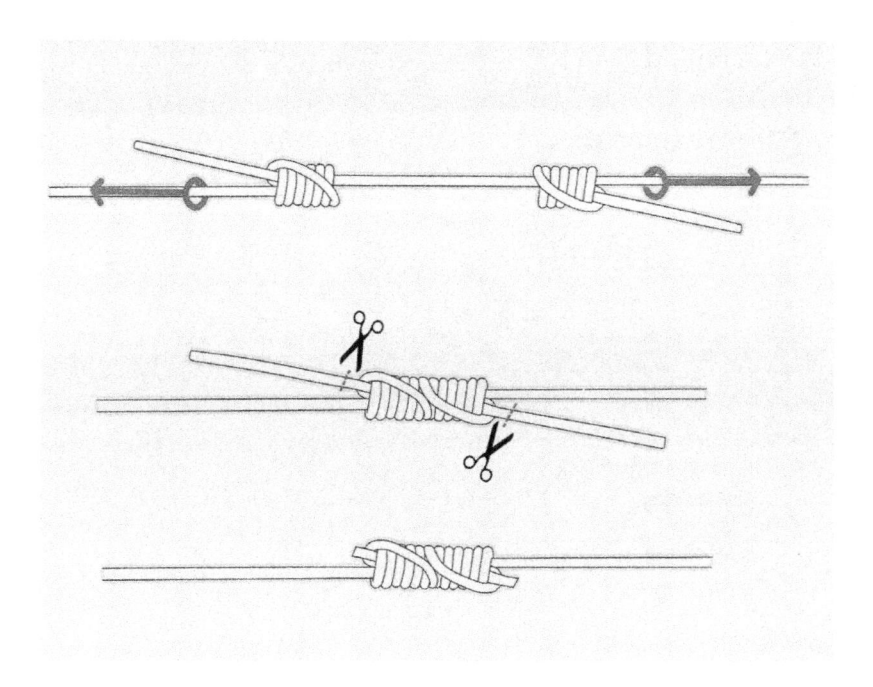

- ✓ Pass the fishing line through the eye of the hook or lure, then double it back to make a loop.

- ✓ Make five turns around the doubled line and through the loop.

- ✓ Wet the knot with water or saliva, then pull the tag end and standing line in opposite directions to tighten the knot.

- ✓ Trim the tag end and standing line close to the knot.

4. Blood Knot

This knot is used to join two pieces of fishing line together.

It is commonly used in fly fishing, where multiple pieces of the line need to be joined.

Step-By-Step Process:

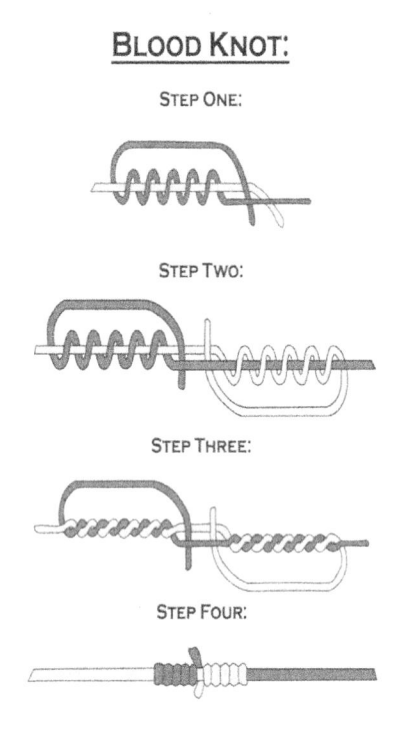

BLOOD KNOT:

STEP ONE:

STEP TWO:

STEP THREE:

STEP FOUR:

- ✓ Overlap the two pieces of line that you want to join. Take the tag end of one of the lines and wrap it around the other line four to six times.

- ✓ Thread the tag end back through the loop created between the two lines.

- ✓ Repeat the process with the other line, wrapping it around the first line four to six times and threading the tag end back through the loop.

- ✓ Wet the knot with water or saliva, then pull the vertical lines in opposite directions to tighten the knot.

- ✓ Trim the tag ends close to the knot.

5. Surgeon's Knot

This knot is used to join two pieces of fishing line together. It is similar to the Blood Knot but is easier to tie and is used for lighter fishing lines.

Step-By-Step Process:

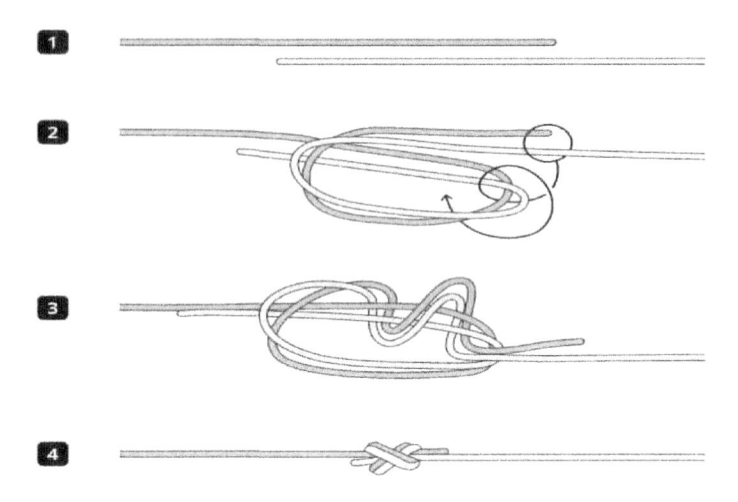

- ✓ Overlap the two pieces of line that you want to join.

- ✓ Tie a simple overhand knot with both lines, but don't tighten it yet.

- ✓ Pass the tag ends and standing lines through the loop twice.

- ✓ Wet the knot with water or saliva, then pull the vertical lines in opposite directions to tighten the knot.

- ✓ Trim the tag ends close to the knot.

Regardless of your knot, the most important thing is to ensure it is solid and secure.

But why?

Let's find out!

• Importance of a Secure and Strong Knot

✓ Secures Your Fish

A strong and secure knot is essential when fishing because it ensures the fish does not escape after being hooked.

On the other hand, a weak knot can break easily, causing the fish to swim away with the hook still in its mouth. This not only results in lost bait but also causes harm to the fish, as it may struggle to eat or swim with the hook in its mouth. Moreover, a weak knot can also lead to lost fishing gear, which is likely costly to replace.

Therefore, tying strong knots is crucial to ensure a successful catch and avoid harm or losses.

✓ Enables Accurate Casting and Control during Fishing

A strong and secure knot also allows for better casting accuracy and overall control of the fishing line. A well-tied knot ensures that the line remains attached to the fishing rod and any movements made by the angler translate smoothly to the lure or bait. This level of control is crucial in fishing as it allows you to manipulate the lure or bait to attract the fish and entice it to bite.

Therefore, taking the time to tie a strong and secure knot increases the chances of a successful catch and provides better control and overall fishing experience.

Chapter Five: Selecting the Right Fishing Spot

You probably feel ready to start fishing after learning how to tie your knots.

But,

Where are you going to fish?

And,

How do you choose the right fishing spot?

This section will answer all these questions and more!

Understanding the Habits and Preferences of Different Types of Fish

Understanding the habits and preferences of different types of fish is essential when choosing the right fishing spot because it increases the chances of a successful catch.

Fish species have **_various preferences_** for water temperature, depth, and habitat, affecting where they are likely to be found. For example, some fish species inhabit shallow waters near the shore, while others prefer deep waters or areas with underwater structures such as rocks, logs, or weed beds.

And,

By understanding these preferences, you can choose a fishing spot likely to be frequented by the desired species.

Moreover, knowing the ***feeding habits*** of different fish species can also help you choose the right fishing spot. Some fish species are predatory and feed on smaller fish or other aquatic creatures, while others are herbivores and feed on plants or insects.

And,

By understanding the feeding habits of different species, you can choose the right bait or lure to attract the desired fish.

Factors to Consider when Choosing a Fishing Spot

1. Water Depth

Various fish species prefer different water depths, meaning some species are more commonly found in shallow water, while others like deep water. It is essential to know the water depth where the fish you are targeting is likely to be to increase the chances of a successful catch.

For example, ***largemouth bass and sunfish*** prefer shallow water with aquatic vegetation and cover, while ***trout and steelhead*** tend to reside in colder, deeper water.

2. Water Temperature

Water temperature affects fish behavior and feeding habits. Some fish prefer cooler water, while others prefer warmer water. For example, **smallmouth bass** tends to be active in warm water, while **salmon** prefer cooler water.

Therefore, knowing the temperature preferences of different fish species can help you determine the best time of year and location to fish.

Here is a table to summarize the different temperature and water depth preferences for various fish species:

Fish Species	Preferred Water Depth	Preferred Water Temperature
Trout	Shallow or Deep	50-60°F (10-15.5°C)
Bass	Shallow or Deep	68-78°F (20-26°C)
Catfish	Deep	70-75°F (21-24°C)
Walleye	Deep	55-68°F (12.8-20°C)
Pike	Shallow or Deep	50-65°F (10-18°C)
Bluegill	Shallow	70-75°F (21-24°C)
Crappie	Shallow or Deep	68-72°F (20-22°C)

Carp	Shallow or Deep	68-72°F (20-22°C)
Redfish	Shallow or Deep	68-78°F (20-26°C)
Flounder	Shallow or Deep	50-65°F (10-18°C)
Swordfish	Deep	70-80°F (21-27°C)
Mahi-mahi	Shallow or Deep	75-85°F (24-29°C)
Tuna	Deep	70-80°F (21-27°C)

3. Water Flow and availability of Water Structures

Some fish species prefer calm, slow-moving water, while others are commonly found in faster-moving water. For example, **catfish** love slower currents, whereas **salmon and trout** are found in faster-moving waters.

Knowing the water flow preferences of different fish species can help you choose the right fishing spot and equipment.

The availability of water structures is also a crucial factor to consider when choosing a fishing spot. Fish gather around **underwater structures** because these structures provide shelter, food, and a sense of security for the fish. For example, **a rocky shoreline** can provide hiding places for small baitfish, attracting larger predator fish. **Fallen trees or logs** in the water can provide shade and shelter for fish, especially during hot summer when the water temperature is higher. **Weed beds** offer a haven for fish to hide, feed and reproduce. These structures create a complex ecosystem that supports the growth and survival of different fish species.

As an angler, knowing the availability of water structure in your chosen fishing spot can help you determine what kind of fish you might catch and what type of bait or lures to use. For instance, if you're fishing around weed beds, using hook-less lures can help prevent getting snagged in the vegetation while also attracting fish feeding in the area.

Below is a table showing different fish species and the type of water conditions they prefer:

Fish Species	Preferred Water Flow/Water Structures.
Trout	Fast-moving water with plenty of oxygen and cover
Bass	Slow to moderate moving water with structure and cover
Walleye	Moderate to fast-moving water with rocky or gravel bottoms

Catfish	Slow-moving water with plenty of cover and structure
Salmon	Fast-moving water with cool temperatures and gravel beds
Pike	Slow to moderate moving water with plenty of structure and cover
Carp	Slow-moving water with soft, muddy bottoms and plenty of vegetation
Crappie	Slow-moving water with plenty of cover and structure
Musky	Moderate to fast-moving water with plenty of cover and structure.

4. Water Clarity

Clear waters are great for sight fishing, unlike murky waters.

Why?

When the water is murky, the visibility reduces, making it more difficult for fish to locate their prey and for anglers to attract them.

It is, therefore, vital to adjust your fishing techniques and equipment accordingly to overcome the challenges posed by murky water.

Here are some tips for what works best in murky water:

✓ ***Use bright or noisy lures***

In murky water, visibility is limited, so using lures that create noise and vibrations can help fish locate your bait.

Brightly colored lures, such as fluorescent or chartreuse, can also help your lure stand out in the murky water.

✓ ***Fish in shallower waters***

Murky water tends to be warmer, so fish often move to shallower waters with more comfortable temperatures. Fishing in shallow water can increase your chances of catching fish as they are more likely to feed and be active in these areas.

✓ ***Try scent-based baits***

In murky water, fish rely heavily on their sense of smell to locate food. Using baits that emit strong scents, such as cut bait or scented plastics, can help attract fish to your line.

Let's look at different fish species and the scents that attract them:

1) **Trout:** Anise, garlic, and salmon egg scents are likely effective in attracting trout.

2) **Bass**: Crawfish, garlic, and shad scents are often used to attract bass.

3) **Walleye**: Nightcrawler, leech, and minnow scents are commonly used to attract walleye.

4) **Catfish**: Blood, chicken liver, and cheese scents effectively attract catfish.

5) **Salmon**: Shrimp, krill, and herring scents are likely used to attract salmon.

6) **Pike**: Smelt, shad, and anise scents can effectively attract pike.

7) **Carp**: Corn, dough, and strawberry scents are commonly used to attract carp.

8) **Crappie**: Shad, minnow, and banana scents are effective in attracting crappie.

9) **Musky:** Sucker, smelt, and anise scents are often used to attract musky.

✓ *Slow down your retrieve*

In murky water, fish may be less active and less likely to chase after a fast-moving lure.

So,

Slowing down your retrieve can give fish more time to locate and strike your bait.

✓ *Experiment with different colors and shapes*

Fish may be more sensitive to specific colors and shapes in murky water.

Experiment with different bait and lure colors, shapes, and sizes to see what works best in the murky water you are fishing.

5. Weather

Different fish behave differently in various weather conditions, as shown by the examples below:

✓ **Trout:** Trout prefer cooler water temperatures and feed more actively on cloudy days. They may also become more aggressive during light rain, which can wash insects into the water.

✓ **Catfish:** Catfish tend to feed more actively during low light conditions, such as early morning, late evening, or cloudy days. They may also be more active during light rain because the rain washes insects and other food sources into the water.

- ✓ **Salmon**: Salmon migrate upstream during rainy weather conditions as it can increase the water levels and make it easier for them to swim.

- ✓ **Crappie:** Crappies tend to prefer sunny days, as they can warm up the water and increase the activity of baitfish. They may also move to shallower waters during a light rain, as it can also attract baitfish.

- ✓ **Bluegill:** Bluegill tends to feed more actively during warm weather conditions and prefers sunny days. They may also become more active during light rain because the rain can wash insects and other food sources into the water.

- ✓ **Bass:** Bass tends to be more active during dawn and dusk or overcast days. They may also become more aggressive during light rain, which can wash insects into the water. Bass also prefer water temperatures between 60-75°F.

- ✓ **Walleye**: Walleyes are more active during low light conditions, such as dawn and dusk, or on overcast days. They also prefer water temperatures between 60-70°F.

- ✓ **Pike**: Pike tends to be more active during dawn and dusk or overcast days. They prefer cooler water temperatures between 50-65°F and may become more active during light rain.

- ✓ **Musky:** Musky tends to be more active during dawn and dusk or overcast days. They prefer cooler water temperatures between 55-70°F and may become more aggressive during light rain.

- ✓ **Tilapia:** Tilapia prefer warm water temperatures between 75-85°F and are more active during daylight hours. They may also become more active during high humidity or rising water temperature periods.

- ✓ **Perch:** Perch tend to be more active during dawn and dusk or overcast days. They prefer water temperatures between 55-65°F and may move to shallower waters during a light rain.

- ✓ **Redfish:** Redfish prefer warmer water temperatures between 70-85°F and are more active during tidal changes. They may also become more active during periods of low light, such as dawn or dusk.

6. Access

Easy access to a fishing spot is essential for safety and convenience. It is crucial to choose a place that is ***safe and accessible***.

Tips for Locating Fish in a New Location

When fishing in an area you've never fished before, or when it's your first time fishing, here are some tips to help you locate fish more easily:

✓ **Observe the Water**

Spend some time observing the water and the surrounding area. Fish often seek cover from predators, and underwater structures provide this.

Therefore, look for underwater structures such as rocks, weed beds, and drop-offs, which can attract fish.

Also, watch for signs of fish activity, such as jumping or feeding fish.

✓ **Follow the Birds**

Seabirds such as gulls and terns can indicate where fish are in saltwater areas.

Why?

These birds feed on the same fish you are targeting, so if you see a group of birds diving into the water, it's a good sign that there are fish below.

✓ Pay Attention to the Current

In moving water, fish tend to face upstream to conserve energy while waiting for food to come to them.

Therefore,

By casting upstream and retrieving your bait downstream, you can mimic the natural flow of food in the water, increasing your chances of a bite.

✓ Ask Locals

Locals familiar with the area can provide valuable insight into where to find fish.

Check with the local bait shops, fishing guides, or even other anglers to learn about the best spots and techniques for the area.

✓ Experiment with Different Techniques

If you're not having any luck with one technique, try something different.

Different fish species and locations may require different approaches, so be willing to experiment until you find what works best.

With all the tips discussed in this chapter, you're ready to start fishing.

And so,

Let's move on to the next chapter and learn about the different types of fishing.

SECTION TWO: DIFFERENT TYPES OF FISHING

As a beginner, you may wonder what fishing types exist and how they differ. Well, wonder no more! In this section, we'll look at the various types of fishing, from the peaceful and patient art of fly fishing to the adrenaline-pumping thrill of big game fishing.

Have you ever tried your hand at ice fishing, where you sit on a frozen lake and jig for hours on end?

What about surf fishing, where you cast your line from the sandy shoreline?

Or maybe you've only ever fished in freshwater lakes and rivers, but have you considered saltwater fishing for more extensive and challenging catches?

There's so much to explore and discover in the world of fishing. And in this section, you will learn the different types of fishing out there to help you find the perfect fit for your interests and skill level.

That said, here are the different types of fishing:

Chapter Six: Fresh Water Fishing

Freshwater fishing is a type of fishing that takes place in bodies of water that contain **little to no salt,** such as lakes, rivers, ponds, and streams. This type of fishing is famous worldwide, and you can enjoy it no matter your skill level.

One of the benefits of freshwater fishing is that you **can do it in many different locations**, ranging from small streams and ponds to large lakes and rivers. Many local parks, wildlife areas, and state or national parks offer opportunities for freshwater fishing, as do private ponds or lakes.

If you're interested in freshwater fishing, an excellent first step is to check out the regulations and guidelines for fishing in your area, including:

- ✓ Obtaining a fishing license or permit.
- ✓ Learning about catch limits and size restrictions.
- ✓ Familiarizing yourself with any specific rules or regulations that apply to the bodies of water where you plan to fish.

Once you're ready to start fishing, you can explore different locations and techniques to find the best for you.

Whether you're a beginner or an experienced angler, freshwater fishing offers plenty of opportunities to enjoy the great outdoors and potentially land some impressive catches.

Different Types of Fresh Water Fish and How to Catch Them

1) Bass

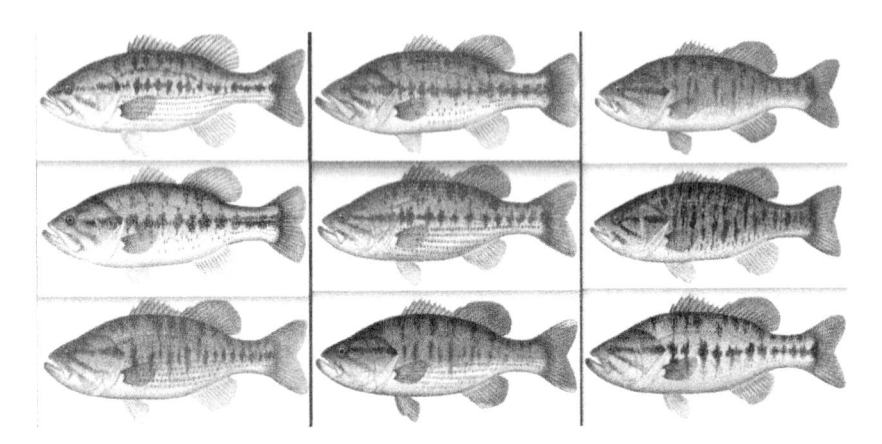

Bass is among many lakes and rivers' most popular freshwater game fish.

Here is how to catch this fish:

To catch bass, try using plastic worms, spinnerbaits, or crankbaits. **Cast your lines** near cover, such as logs or vegetation, and vary your retrieve speed to entice the fish to strike.

2) Trout

Trout are often found in cold, clear streams and rivers.

And how do you can them?

Use small lures or flies, such as spinners, spoons, or nymphs, to catch trout. Please **pay attention to the current** and try to present your bait or fly so that it drifts naturally with the flow.

3) Panfish

Panfish, such as bluegill, crappie, and perch, are likely found in many freshwater bodies of water.

To catch panfish,

Use small hooks and bait, such as worms or small nightcrawler pieces. **Cast your lines** near cover or structure, such as weeds or fallen trees, and be patient, as panfish may take some time to find your bait.

4) Pike

Pike are predatory fish likely to be found in many freshwater lakes and rivers.

To catch pike,

Use large spoons, swimbaits, or live bait, such as minnows or suckers. **Cast your line** near weed beds or drop-offs and vary your retrieve speed to entice the fish to strike.

5) Catfish

Catfish are often found in muddy rivers or lakes.

To catch them,

You can use a variety of bait, such as worms, stink bait, or cut bait. **Cast your lines** near structure or cover, such as logs or rocks, and be patient, as catfish may take some time to find your bait.

6) Musky

Musky, or muskellunge, are large, elusive fish often sought by experienced anglers.

***To catch musky*,**

Try using large crankbaits, spinnerbaits, or live bait such as suckers or chubs. ***Cast your line*** near weed beds or rocky areas, and be patient, as musky may take some time to strike.

7) Salmon

Salmon are often found in large rivers or the Great Lakes.

To catch salmon,

Try using flies that imitate their natural prey, such as smelt or alewives. Please pay attention to the current and try to present your lure or fly so that it drifts naturally with the flow.

8) Carp

Carp are often found in large, slow-moving rivers or lakes.

And how do you catch carp fish?

Use dough balls or corn as bait or a small jig or fly to catch carp. **Cast your line** near the bottom of the water and be patient, as carp are likely finicky and may take some time to find your bait.

9) Walleye

Walleye are predatory fish likely to be found in many freshwater lakes and rivers.

To catch walleye,

Try using jigs or crankbaits that imitate their natural prey, such as minnows or crayfish. **Cast your line** near drop-offs or rocky areas and vary your retrieve speed to entice the fish to strike.

Gear and Equipment for Fresh Water Fishing

Freshwater fishing requires different equipment depending on the type and size of fish you plan to catch.

Here are some specific examples to help you choose the right gear:

- ✓ **Rod**

The size and strength of the rod should match the size of the fish you plan to catch. For example, a light or ultralight rod would be appropriate to target smaller fish like bluegill or crappie. However, you'll need a medium or medium-heavy rod to go after larger fish like bass or pike.

Rods are often labeled with a weight rating, such as the "4-10 lb test," which indicates the range of line weight the rod is designed to handle.

- ✓ **Reel**

The reel should match the size of the rod, and it should also have a drag system that can handle the weight of the fish you're targeting. For smaller fish, a spinning reel would be appropriate, while for larger fish, a baitcasting reel may be necessary.

Reels are often labeled with a weight rating, such as the "6-12 lb test," which indicates the range of line weight the reel is designed to handle.

✓ Line

The size and strength of the line should also match the size of the fish you're targeting. For example, if you're targeting small panfish, you might use a 2-6 lb test monofilament line. However, if you're targeting larger fish like bass or catfish, you might use a 10-20 lb test line.

Remember that different types of lines have various properties - for example, a braided line is firm and sensitive but is likely visible in clear water. In contrast, a fluorocarbon line is nearly invisible but is probably more expensive.

Techniques for Fresh Water Fishing

Here are a few techniques you can use to catch freshwater fish without too much hassle:

1. Casting and Retrieving

The casting and retrieving fishing technique is fundamental and is commonly used in freshwater fishing.

What does it entail?

It involves throwing your lure or bait into the water using a rod and reel and reeling it back in. This technique imitates the movement of a swimming prey, which can attract fish to bite.

It would be best to start by casting out your bait or lure into the water by pulling back the rod and then quickly flicking it forward. This motion sends your lure or bait flying through the air and into the water. After your bait or lure hits the water, you can retrieve it by turning the handle on your reel.

As you reel in your bait or lure, you want to imitate the natural movement of swimming prey. You can achieve this movement by varying the depth and speed of your retrieve. For example, you can speed up your retrieve to make your lure or bait look like it's trying to escape from a predator or slow it down to make it look more like a wounded fish.

Varying the depth of your retrieve can also be effective. You can retrieve your bait or lure close to the surface if fishing in shallow water. However, if you're fishing in deeper water, you may need to let your bait or lure sink deeper before starting your retrieve.

2. Bottom Fishing

Bottom fishing involves fishing on or near the water bottom, where many species of fish feed.

How?

You can use a sinker or weight to keep your bait near the bottom and wait for a fish to fall for the bait.

3. Fly Fishing

This technique uses a unique weighted line and a lightweight rod to cast a small, weightless fly out into the water.

This technique is effective, especially for catching trout and other fish species that feed on insects and small prey.

4. Trolling

Trolling involves fishing from a moving boat, slowly dragging your bait or lure behind you as you move through the water.

This technique is likely ideal for catching larger, more aggressive fish like musky and pike.

Remember, the key to successful freshwater fishing is patience, persistence, and willingness to experiment with different techniques and baits until you find what works.

Let's move on to the next chapter and learn about another type of fishing.

Chapter Seven: Salt Water Fishing

Saltwater fishing *is recreational or commercial fishing* done in oceans, seas, or other bodies of saltwater. It involves catching a wide range of saltwater fish species using various methods such as angling, trolling, netting, trapping, or spearfishing. Saltwater fishing is done from shore or a boat and is practiced for several reasons, such as sports, food, or commerce.

Saltwater fishing is done in many locations worldwide, as long as there is access to saltwater bodies. **Some popular saltwater fishing destinations include** the Florida Keys, the Gulf of Mexico, the Caribbean, Hawaii, the Mediterranean, the Great Barrier Reef in Australia, and the coasts of South Africa and South America.

- **Different Types of Salt Water Fish and How to Catch Them**

These are some of the species you are likely to find when fishing in salty waters:

1. Tuna

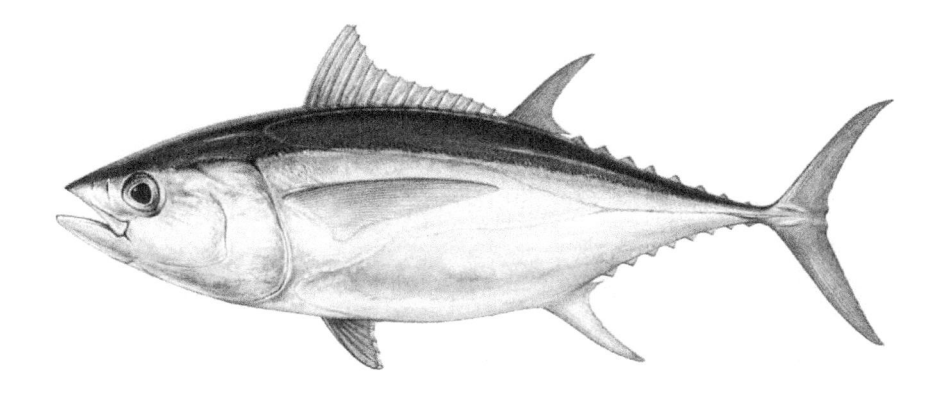

When fishing for Tuna, two popular techniques are trolling and chunking.

To use the trolling technique:

- ✓ First, you need to locate an area where you are likely to find Tuna, such as near a school of baitfish.

- ✓ Once you have identified the area, set up your trolling rig with a heavy-duty rod and reel, and attach a trolling lure or bait to your line.

- ✓ Start trolling slowly and adjust your speed and lure depth based on the behavior of the tuna.

- ✓ When a Tuna strikes, reel in quickly and set the hook firmly to ensure a successful catch.

Trolling is an effective way to catch Tuna as it allows you to cover a lot of water and mimic the movement of baitfish.

And how do you use the chunking fishing technique?

Chunking involves using small pieces of baitfish, such as mackerel or squid, to attract Tuna to your fishing area.

To use the chunking technique:

- ✓ Start by chumming the water with small pieces of baitfish to create a scent trail that will attract Tuna.

- ✓ Once attracted to the area, cast your baited hook with a small piece of baitfish and wait for a bite.

- ✓ When a Tuna takes the bait, reel it in quickly and set the hook firmly to ensure a successful catch.

Chunking is an effective technique when fishing for Tuna, especially in areas where Tuna are known to be present but are not actively feeding on the surface.

2. Marlin

Marlin is another highly prized game fish that is caught using *trolling techniques*.

To catch marlin fish:

Use lures that mimic the marlin's preferred prey, such as squid or flying fish, and vary your trolling speed to create a more natural presentation.

3. Swordfish

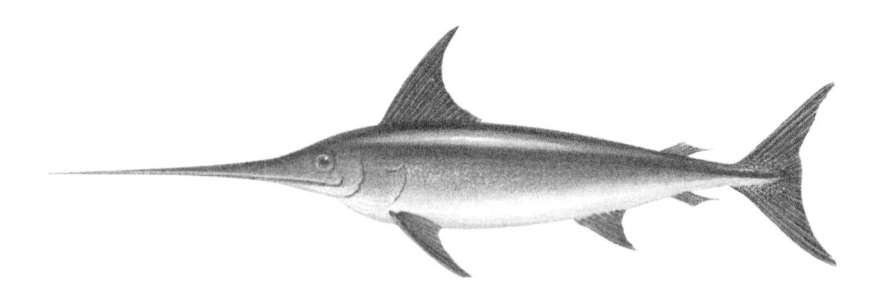

Swordfish is caught using **deep-dropping techniques**, where you drop bait or lures to depths of several hundred feet.

Use baits that emit light, such as squid or glowing jigs, to attract swordfish to your bait.

4. Grouper

Grouper are caught using **bottom fishing techniques**.

Here is how to catch grouper fish:

Drop bait to the bottom and wait for the grouper to take the bait, then reel in slowly to avoid the fish retreating into its hole. Use heavy tackle and a large, sturdy hook to handle the grouper's powerful bite.

5. Snapper

Snappers are also caught using **bottom fishing techniques**.

To catch these fish:

Use smaller hooks and lighter tackle than you would for grouper, and drop bait to the bottom. Snappers are known to be wary of hooks, so be patient and wait for the fish to fully take the bait before setting the hook.

6. Barracuda

Barracuda caught using **casting or trolling techniques**.

Use lures that imitate small fish and vary your retrieve speed to create a more natural presentation. Barracuda have sharp teeth, so **use a wire leader** to prevent the fish from cutting your line.

- ## Salt Water Fishing Gear

Here are the items you'll need for saltwater fishing:

✓ **Saltwater Fishing Rod and Reel**

Saltwater rods and reels are typically more extensive and durable than their freshwater counterparts. They are designed to handle the bigger, stronger fish commonly found in saltwater environments.

✓ **Saltwater Fishing Line**

Saltwater fishing line is thicker and more robust than freshwater line and is designed to withstand the corrosive effects of saltwater.

✓ **Saltwater Fishing Lures and Baits**

Saltwater fishing lures and baits are designed to mimic the natural prey of saltwater fish, such as squid, shrimp, and baitfish. They are typically more extensive and more colorful than freshwater lures.

✓ **Saltwater Fishing Hooks**

Saltwater fishing hooks are made of corrosion-resistant materials such as stainless steel and are designed to handle the bigger, stronger fish commonly found in saltwater environments.

✓ **Saltwater Fishing Leaders**

As discussed earlier, saltwater fishing leaders are made of heavy-duty monofilament or wire and are used to prevent the fish from biting through the fishing line.

✓ **Saltwater Fishing Tackle Box**

A tackle box for saltwater fishing should be made of durable, waterproof materials and contain various lures, baits, hooks, and leaders.

✓ **Saltwater Fishing Waders or Boots**

Saltwater fishing often involves wading in shallow water, so it is important to have waterproof waders or boots capable of keeping your feet dry.

✓ **Saltwater Fishing Net**

It would help if you had a saltwater fishing net when fishing in saltwater because it is specifically designed to withstand the corrosive effects of saltwater. The high salt content in the water can cause damage to regular fishing nets, making them weaker and more prone to breakage.

Saltwater nets are typically made from materials resistant to corrosion, such as nylon or rubber-coated mesh, and have reinforced handles and frames to provide extra strength and durability. In addition to their durability, saltwater fishing nets have larger mesh sizes and deeper bags, making them better suited for catching larger saltwater species.

- **Techniques for Saltwater Fishing**

There are many techniques for saltwater fishing, each designed to catch different types of fish in different environments.

Here are several techniques for saltwater fishing and how they work:

1. Trolling

This saltwater fishing technique entails **dragging your bait or lures** behind a moving boat to attract fish.

This technique is popular for catching game fish such as ***marlin, tuna, and sailfish***.

When fishing, the speed of the boat and the type of lure or bait used will depend on the target species.

2. Bottom Fishing

This technique entails **dropping a lure or bait at the bottom of the ocean** to attract fish near the bottom.

This technique is popular for catching ***grouper, snapper, and halibut*** species.

The type of bait and hook used will depend on the target species and the water depth.

3. Jigging

The jigging technique entails releasing weighted baits or lures to the bottom of the ocean floor and then jerking it upward and downward to allure fish.

This technique is popular for catching **tuna, amberjack, and snapper** species.

The weight of the lure and the speed and motion of the jig will depend on the target species.

4. Surf Fishing

Surf fishing involves ***fishing from the shoreline*** or wading into the surf to catch fish.

This technique is popular for catching ***striped bass, redfish, and bluefish***.

The type of bait and hook used will depend on the target species and the time of year.

5. Fly Fishing

Fly fishing involves casting **a lightweight artificial fly** to attract fish.

This technique is popular for catching **bonefish, tarpon, and permit** species.

The type of fly used will depend on the target species and the conditions of the water.

6. Live Bait Fishing

Live bait fishing involves using live bait, such as shrimp, squid, or small fish, which attract your target catch.

This technique is popular for catching various species and is often used when other methods are not working.

The type of bait used will depend on the target species.

These are just a few of the many techniques for saltwater fishing. Each method requires different gear and equipment and knowledge of the target species and their behaviors.

In the next chapter, we will discuss another type of fishing known as fly fishing.

Chapter Eight: Fly Fishing

This fishing technique uses a specialized fishing line, reel, and rod to cast a manufactured fly. This fly is designed to mimic the natural prey of the target fish, such as insects or small fish. The goal of fly fishing is to present the fly in an attractive way to the fish, enticing them to bite.

And where can you practice fly fishing?

Fly fishing technique is done in many places, including rivers, lakes, and saltwater flats. Some of the most popular locations for fly fishing include trout streams, salmon rivers, and mountain streams. **Trout streams** are prevalent for fly fishing, as they offer some of the best opportunities to catch trout using this technique. In saltwater, fly fishing is often done **on shallow flats** where bonefish, tarpon, and other species are likely found. Fly fishing in **still water**, such as on lakes and ponds, is also popular and can offer the opportunity to catch various species, including bass and panfish.

Overall, fly fishing is a versatile and enjoyable form of fishing practiced in many places and for many different fish species. It requires specialized gear and techniques, but with practice, it is a highly effective and rewarding way to catch fish.

1. Different Flies and Lures

Various flies and lures are used in fly fishing, each designed to mimic different types of natural prey and attract multiple fish species.

Here are some of the most common types of flies and lures used in fly fishing:

- **Dry Flies**

Dry flies are designed to float on the water's surface and mimic insects such as mayflies, caddisflies, and grasshoppers.

They are often used in ***trout fishing*** and are very effective for catching fish when they are feeding on the surface.

- **Nymphs**

Nymphs are designed to imitate aquatic insects such as mayfly nymphs, stonefly nymphs, and caddisfly larvae.

They are fished below the water's surface and are particularly effective *in slow-moving or still-water environments.*

- **Streamers**

Streamers are designed to imitate small fish, leeches, and other aquatic creatures.

They often ***target larger fish*** such as trout, bass, and pike and are fished by stripping the line through the water.

- **Wet Flies**

Wet flies, like tiny insects or baitfish, are designed to sink and move through the water.

They are fished at different depths and are often used in ***trout and salmon fishing***.

- **Terrestrial Flies**

Terrestrial flies imitate insects that live on land, such as beetles and grasshoppers. They are often *used in late summer and fall* when insects are blown onto the water.

- **Saltwater Flies**

Saltwater flies are designed to mimic small baitfish, shrimp, and other prey species found in saltwater environments. They often target species such as **bonefish, tarpon, and striped bass.**

Overall, the selection of fly or lure will depend on your target fish and the water conditions.

Experienced fly fishermen often carry a variety of flies and lure with them to ensure they have the right one for the situation. So, when fishing, bring several flies and lures to experiment until you find what works.

2. What is the Right Gear and Equipment for Fly Fishing?

Fly fishing is a popular fishing method that requires specialized gear and equipment. The right gear is essential for fly fishing, as it helps you to catch fish more efficiently and effectively.

The primary equipment for fly fishing is ***a fly rod***, which is typically longer and more flexible than traditional fishing rods.

Why is it so?

The length and flexibility of the rod allow you to cast a lightweight artificial fly with precision and accuracy.

Fly rods are available in different sizes and weights, depending on the size of the fish and the type of water being fished.

A fly reel is also needed to hold the fly line attached to the fly rod. In addition to the fly rod and reel, other essential fly fishing gear includes a fly line, leader, tippet, and artificial flies. ***The fly line*** is o be lightweight and tapered, allowing it to be cast precisely and accurately. ***The leader and tippet*** are used to connect the fly line to the fly, and they are typically made from clear monofilament or fluorocarbon. ***Artificial flies*** are available in various designs and sizes, and they mimic the appearance and behavior of natural insects or other small aquatic creatures.

Other gears useful for fly fishing include ***waders, a vest or chest pack, polarized sunglasses, and a landing net***.

Using the right gear and equipment can increase their chances of success and enjoy a more enjoyable and productive fishing experience.

3. Techniques of Fly Fishing

Here are some of the most common techniques used in fly fishing:

- ✓ **Dry Fly Fishing**

This technique involves fishing with a floating fly on the water's surface, imitating an insect or other small creature.

This method is ideal for fishing in **calm water**, where fish feed on the surface.

✓ **Wet Fly Fishing**

This technique involves fishing with a fly submerged in the water, imitating a nymph or other underwater creature.

This method is best suited for fishing in **moving water**, where fish feed below the surface.

✓ **Streamer Fishing**

This technique involves fishing with a large, brightly colored fly that imitates a baitfish or larger prey.

This method is ideal for fishing in rivers or streams with ***fast-moving water***.

✓ **Nymphing**

This technique involves fishing with a weighted fly that imitates an underwater insect or other small creature.

This method is typically used in ***slower-moving water***, such as streams or small rivers.

✓ **Euro Nymphing**

This specialized nymphing technique involves fishing with a long, thin fly line and a heavily weighted fly.

This method is ideal for fishing in *fast-moving water*, where traditional nymphing techniques may not be effective.

✓ **Spey Casting**

This casting technique uses a more extended, two-handed fly rod to make long, elegant casts.

This method is ideal for fishing in *large rivers* or using heavier flies.

By experimenting with different techniques, you can increase your chances of success and find the most effective method for the water and fish species you are targeting.

4. List of Fish Caught Through Fly Fishing

Fly fishing method is used to catch the following fish species:

- Trout (Rainbow, Brown, Brook, Cutthroat, etc.)
- Salmon (Chinook, Coho, Sockeye, Atlantic, etc.)
- Steelhead
- Bass (Largemouth, Smallmouth)
- Panfish (Bluegill, Crappie, Sunfish, etc.)

- Pike
- Musky
- Carp
- Bonefish
- Tarpon
- Permit
- Redfish
- Snook
- Striped Bass
- Grayling
- Arctic Char
- Grayling
- Shad
- Walleye
- Catfish

Let's now move to the next chapter and learn about boat fishing.

Chapter Nine: Boat Fishing

Boat fishing is a recreational activity that involves catching fish while on a boat. This type of fishing offers a unique experience you cannot replicate by shore fishing.

Here is how:

- ✓ Boat fishing allows you to explore different bodies of water and reach inaccessible areas from the shore.

- ✓ It also is an excellent opportunity to catch larger fish not usually found near the coast.

- ✓ You can practice boat fishing in various types of water, including lakes, rivers, streams, and oceans. You can do this activity alone, with friends, or with family, making it a perfect way to spend time outdoors and create lasting memories.

There are many places where you can enjoy boat fishing.

For example,

- ✓ **_Lakes and reservoirs_** are popular destinations for anglers who prefer **_calm waters_**, while river fishing is ideal for anglers who like challenges because the currents offer precisely that.

- ✓ In addition, **_saltwater fishing_** is a favorite among anglers who enjoy the thrill of catching **_large game fish_**, such as marlin, tuna, and shark.

Many countries have established fishing charters that provide anglers with boats, equipment, and guides to ensure a successful fishing trip. Additionally, many public and private lakes and rivers allow anglers to bring their boats, providing more flexibility and freedom to explore the water.

Whether you're a beginner or an angler looking for more experience, boat fishing is a fun and exciting way to connect with nature and catch fish.

Gear and Equipment Needed for Boat Fishing

You will need various gear and equipment to enjoy a successful boat fishing experience.

Firstly, you will need ***a fishing rod and reel*** designed for the type of fish you are targeting. For instance, if you're fishing for larger fish such as tuna or shark, you will need a heavy-duty rod and reel that can handle the weight and strength of these fish.

Secondly, you will need ***a tackle box*** filled with hooks, lines, and sinkers. The tackle box should also include lures and bait suitable for the type of fish you are targeting.

In addition to fishing gear, you will also need ***boating equipment*** to ensure your safety and comfort. This includes a life jacket or personal floatation device (PFD), which is mandatory in many countries. You will also need an anchor to keep the boat in place while you fish and a navigation system, such as a GPS or a chart, to help you navigate the water.

It's necessary to pack enough water and food for your trip, as well as a first aid kit in case of emergencies. Other essential items include sunscreen, a hat, sunglasses to protect you from the sun, and a cooler to store your catch and snacks.

You can enjoy a comfortable and successful boat fishing experience by being well-prepared and having the right gear.

Techniques for Boat Fishing

There are various fishing techniques that you can use for successful boat fishing, depending on the type of fish you are targeting and the body of water you are fishing in.

Here are some of the most common techniques:

- **Trolling**

This involves dragging bait or lures behind the boat slowly to attract fish.

Trolling is an effective technique for catching game fish such as tuna and marlin.

- **Bottom Fishing**

This technique involves dropping bait to the bottom of the water and waiting for fish to bite.

It is suitable for catching bottom-dwelling fish such as grouper, snapper, and cod.

- **Jigging**

This technique uses a weighted lure bounced up and down to attract fish.

Jigging is a popular technique for catching fish such as bass and walleye.

- **Casting**

This technique involves casting bait or lures to a specific spot to attract fish.

Casting is a versatile technique used in various types of water and is effective for catching a wide range of fish species.

- **Fly Fishing**

This technique involves using a lightweight fly rod and artificial flies to mimic the movement of insects or small fish.

Fly fishing is suitable for catching trout, salmon, and other freshwater fish.

By mastering these techniques, you can increase your chances of catching fish and have a successful boat fishing experience.

Popular Fish Caught Through Boat Fishing

You can catch the following fish species when boat fishing:

- Tuna (Yellowfin, Bluefin, Albacore, etc.)
- Marlin (Blue, White, Striped)

- Sailfish
- Mahi-mahi (Dorado)
- Wahoo
- Snapper (Red, Yellowtail, Lane, etc.)
- Grouper (Gag, Red, Black, etc.)
- Amberjack
- Cobia
- Barracuda
- King Mackerel
- Tarpon
- Shark
- Halibut
- Lingcod
- Rockfish
- Salmon (Chinook, Coho, Sockeye, etc.)
- Trout (Rainbow, Brown, Lake, etc.)

- Walleye

- Catfish

Let's now look at surf fishing in the next chapter.

Chapter Ten: Surf Fishing

Surf fishing is a type of fishing that involves casting a line from the shore into the ocean's surf zone, where the waves break. This type of fishing will be great for you if you prefer **the beach** and want to catch fish such as striped bass, bluefish, and flounder.

Surf fishing requires specific equipment, including a longer rod and reel designed for distance casting, heavier tackle to withstand the waves, and baits or lures that imitate the local baitfish. You will also need to be mindful of the tide and waves and any regulations and restrictions in your fishing area.

Surf fishing is done on many beaches worldwide with fish populations, including the United States, Australia, New Zealand, and South Africa. In the United States, popular destinations for surf fishing include the beaches of the Outer Banks in North Carolina, Montauk in New York, and the beaches of Southern California. In Australia, surf fishing is popular on Queensland and New South Wales beaches, while in South Africa, anglers can fish on Cape Town and Durban beaches.

Surf fishing offers a unique and exciting way to connect with nature and catch fish from the beach.

Different Types of Fish Caught Through Surf Fishing and Tips on How to Catch Them

Surf fishing provides you with a wide range of fish species to target. The types of fish caught through surf fishing can vary depending on the region, season, and fishing techniques used.

Here are some of the most common fish species caught through surf fishing, along with tips for catching them:

- **Striped Bass**

Striped bass is a popular game fish caught in the Northeastern United States, from Maine to Virginia. They are known for their size and fighting ability.

You can use a variety of lures and baits, including bucktails, soft plastics, and live eels, to catch striped bass. Fishing during the early morning or evening hours, when the fish are more active, can increase your chances of catching them.

- **Bluefish**

Bluefish are predatory fish found along the Atlantic Coast of the United States, from Maine to Florida. They are known for their sharp teeth and hard-fighting ability.

You can use a variety of lures, such as metal spoons and plugs, to catch bluefish. A wire leader is essential to prevent the fish from cutting the line with their teeth.

- **Redfish**

Redfish or **red drum** is a well-known game fish along the Gulf Coast of the United States, from Texas to Florida. They are known for their bronze color and distinctive black spot on their tail.

You can catch them using a variety of baits, including live shrimp and crabs, to catch redfish. Fishing around oyster beds and other structures can increase your chances of catching them.

- **Surf Perch**

Surf perch are a popular fish species found along the Pacific Coast of the United States, from Alaska to California. They are known for their tasty meat and fighting ability.

You can use various baits, such as sand crabs and bloodworms, to catch surf perch. Fishing during the incoming tide can increase your chances of catching them.

- **Pompano**

Pompano is a popular game fish found along the Atlantic Coast of the United States, from Virginia to Florida. They are known for their excellent eating quality and fast-swimming ability.

You can use a variety of baits, including sand fleas and shrimp, to catch pompano. Fishing during the early morning or evening hours, when the fish are more active, can increase your chances of catching them.

These are just a few examples of the many fish species you can catch through surf fishing. It's essential to research the specific fish species in the area you plan to fish and to use the appropriate gear and techniques to increase your chances of success.

Gear and Equipment Needed for Surf Fishing

Surf fishing requires specific gear and equipment to be successful.

The primary equipment for surf fishing includes a fishing rod, reel, and line. *A spinning reel* is the most common type of reel used for surf fishing due to its ability to hold a lot of lines and withstand the saltwater environment. It would be best if you used a *9 to 12 feet rod* to cast farther into the surf zone. *The fishing line should be strong* enough to handle the weight of the bait and the fish, typically ranging from 15 to 30-pound test.

Additional gear needed includes sinkers, hooks, and bait. **Sinkers** are required to keep the bait on the bottom and to help cast further into the surf zone. **Hooks** come in various sizes, depending on the type of bait used and the size of the fish targeted. Lastly, you need to choose *the right bait or lure* for the species of fish you are targeting. Sand crabs, bloodworms, shrimp, and various lures are popular choices for surf fishing.

Waders or waterproof boots are also recommended to keep you dry while fishing in the surf zone.

Techniques for Surf Fishing

You can do surf fishing using the following techniques:

- **Casting**

This is the most basic technique for surf fishing. You'll want to cast your line into the surf to where the fish are. The further out you can cast, the better your chances of catching fish.

- **Bottom Fishing**

This technique involves casting your line out and letting it sit on the bottom. You'll want to use a weight to keep your bait on the bottom and wait for the fish to come to you.

This technique is suitable for catching bottom-dwelling fish such as flounder and halibut.

- **Surf Rigs**

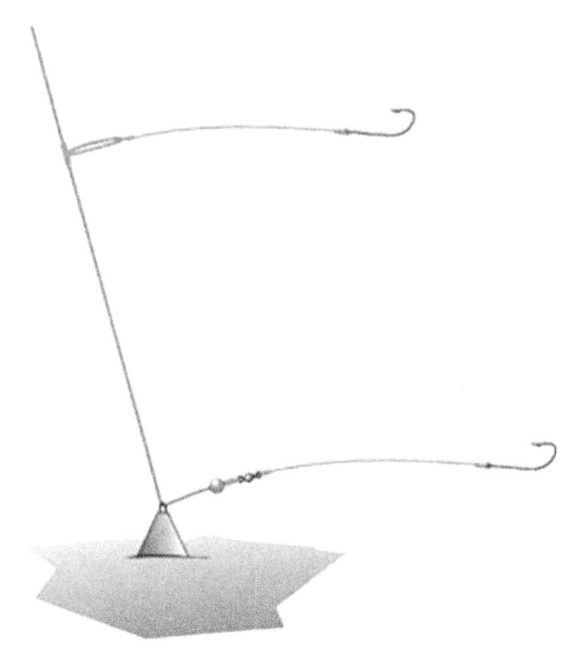

Surf rigs are specialized fishing rigs designed for surf fishing. They typically have multiple hooks and are designed to catch various fish species. Surf rigs are used for casting or bottom fishing.

- **Lure Fishing**

Lure fishing involves using artificial lures to attract fish. You'll want to cast your bait out into the surf and retrieve it in a way that mimics the movements of the fish's natural prey.

- **Live Bait Fishing**

Live bait fishing involves using live bait such as sand crabs, clams, or worms to attract fish. You'll want to cast your bait into the surf and let it sit until a fish takes it.

- **Sight Fishing**

Sight fishing is a technique that involves spotting fish in the surf and casting your line out to them. This is likely more challenging than other techniques, but it is rewarding when you catch a fish you've spotted yourself.

Remember, surf fishing is a bit more challenging than other types of fishing, but it can also be gratifying. Experiment with different techniques and find what works best for you.

Have you heard about kayak fishing? Well, let's explore it in the next chapter.

Chapter Eleven: Kayak Fishing

Kayak fishing is a popular method that involves using *a kayak* as a means of transportation to access fishing spots that may be difficult or impossible to reach by foot or boat. Kayaks used for fishing are typically designed with features such as rod holders, anchor systems, and storage compartments to accommodate fishing gear and catch.

Usually, you paddle or pedal your kayaks to where you will likely find fish and cast your lines from the kayak. Kayak fishing offers a unique and immersive experience, allowing you to get close to nature and enjoy the peacefulness of being on the water.

You can practice kayak fishing in various locations, including lakes, rivers, and oceans. Many anglers prefer to fish in **smaller bodies of water**, such as ponds or small lakes, where the shallow depth and calm waters make it easier to maneuver the kayak and spot fish. However, you can also do kayak fishing in **larger bodies of water**, such as the ocean or large rivers, where anglers target larger species, such as sharks or salmon. Some kayak anglers even participate in **offshore fishing tournaments**, competing against other anglers to catch the biggest fish.

In other words, you can enjoy kayak fishing in almost any body of water with fish, making it a versatile and accessible form of fishing.

Different Types of Fish Caught Through Kayak Fishing

Kayak fishing is an exciting way to catch various fish species.

Here are some of the most popular types of fish that you can catch while kayak fishing, along with some tips and tricks for catching them:

1. Bass

Bass is a widespread fish species caught in fresh and saltwater. They are often found near structures such as docks, rocks, and submerged vegetation.

How do you catch this fish through kayak fishing?

You can catch bass using various baits, including worms, jigs, and topwater lures. Try using a slow retrieve when fishing with jigs or soft plastics and a quick retrieve with topwater lures to create a realistic action that mimics prey.

2. Trout

Trout is a freshwater fish in streams, rivers, and lakes.

To allure and catch trout,

Use bait and lures, including live spinners, baits, and flies. When fishing for trout, try to locate areas with moving water, such as riffles and eddies, where trout tend to feed. Use a light line and a slow retrieve to entice these elusive fish.

3. Redfish

Redfish, or **red drum**, is a saltwater species found along the Atlantic coast and in the Mexican Gulf. They are often found near oyster beds and other structures in shallow water.

You can catch red drums using live bait such as shrimp and mullet and artificial lures such as spoons and soft plastics. Try using a slow retrieve when fishing with soft plastics and a steady retrieve with spoons.

4. Snook

Snook is a saltwater species found in Florida and other tropical waters. They are often found near mangrove shorelines and other structures.

To catch snook using kayak fishing,

Use live bait such as shrimp and pinfish and artificial lures such as topwater plugs and soft plastics. When fishing for snook, try using a slow retrieve with soft plastics and a fast retrieve with topwater plugs to trigger strikes.

5. Catfish

Catfish are freshwater species found in lakes and rivers throughout North America.

They are often located near the bottom of the water column, and you can catch them using live bait, such as worms and stink bait, as well as artificial lures, such as soft plastics and jigs. When fishing for catfish, use a heavy line and a bottom rig to keep your bait near the bottom.

What Gear and Equipment Do You Need for Kayak Fishing?

Kayak fishing requires specialized gear and equipment to ensure a safe and enjoyable experience on the water.

Firstly, you'll need ***a kayak*** specifically designed for fishing, as it typically has rod holders, a comfortable seat, and storage options for your gear. You'll also need ***a paddle*** to propel your kayak through the water.

For fishing, you'll need a ***fishing rod and reel***, along with an appropriate ***fishing line and terminal tackle*** such as hooks, weights, and lures. ***A fish finder*** is likely helpful in locating fish and structures.

Personal safety equipment such as ***a life jacket and whistle*** are also essential.

Other essential items include a dry bag to keep your gear dry, sunscreen, a hat, and polarized sunglasses to reduce glare on the water. Depending on your fishing conditions, you may also need waders, a rain jacket, and insect repellent.

With the right gear and equipment, kayak fishing is a fun and rewarding way to enjoy the outdoors and catch various fish species.

Techniques for Kayak Fishing

Kayak fishing requires a different set of techniques compared to other forms of fishing due to the unique challenges of being in small, maneuverable watercraft.

One of the essential techniques is **_learning how to paddle effectively_**, allowing you to creep through the water without scaring off fish. When you approach an area where you suspect fish may be, such as near structures or drop-offs, try to position yourself in a way that allows you to cast while keeping your kayak stable.

In addition, it's essential to **_learn how to control your kayak_** in different wind and water conditions, as this will help you stay in position and focus on fishing.

Another vital technique is to **_be patient and observant_**, reading the water and watching for signs of fish activity such as surface disturbances, birds feeding, or baitfish jumping.

Finally, **_practicing good catch-and-release techniques_** is crucial to ensure that fish populations remain healthy and sustainable for future generations.

With these techniques and some practice, you can increase your chances of success while kayaking and fishing and enjoy the unique thrill of catching fish from small, nimble watercraft.

Let's move on to the next chapter and learn about bank fishing.

Chapter Twelve: Bank Fishing

Bank fishing refers to fishing from **the shore or riverbank** rather than a boat or kayak. It is a popular and accessible form of fishing that people of all ages and skill levels enjoy.

Depending on the type of fish you are targeting, you can do bank fishing in various locations, including rivers, lakes, ponds, and even the ocean. Some popular spots for bank fishing include public fishing piers, jetties, and parks with access to water.

Bank fishing is a great way to enjoy the outdoors and catch various fish species without requiring specialized equipment or a boat. With some research and preparation, bank fishing is likely a fun and rewarding way to experience the thrill of the catch.

The Different Types of Fish Caught Through Bank Fishing

- **Bass**

Bass is predatory fish caught using lures that mimic their prey, such as spinnerbaits or soft plastic worms. **Look for areas with structure**, such as fallen trees or rocks, where bass may hide and wait to ambush their prey. Cast your lure near these structures and retrieve it slowly and steadily.

Another effective technique is to **"jig" the lure** by bouncing it off the bottom and then pausing, mimicking a wounded or injured fish. Remember that bass is often most active during low-light hours, such as early or late evenings.

- **Catfish**

Catfish are bottom-dwelling fish caught using bait such as chicken liver or nightcrawlers. Fish near the water bottom column in **areas with a strong current or near drop-off**, where catfish are likely to feed.

Be patient, as catfish can take their time to bite, so leaving your bait in the water for an extended period is essential. Use a slip sinker rig, as it lets the catfish fall for the bait without noticing the sinker's weight. When you feel a bite, wait a few seconds before setting the hook to ensure the catfish has fully taken the bait.

- **Panfish (bluegill and crappie)**

Panfish are small freshwater fish caught using small jigs or live bait such as worms or crickets. Fish in ***underwater structures or areas with vegetation*** because panfish may be feeding there. Look for drop-offs or underwater ledges, as panfish like to congregate in these areas.

Cast your bait near the structure and retrieve it slowly and steadily. Remember that panfish have small mouths, so use small hooks and light lines to avoid spooking them.

- **Trout**

Trout are cold-water fish caught using small spinners or flies. They are often found in streams and rivers with ***clear and calm water with good flow***. Look for areas with underwater structures, such as rocks or fallen trees, where trout may be hiding.

Cast your lure upstream and allow it to drift naturally downstream, mimicking the movement of natural prey. When using flies, try to "match the hatch" by using a fly that imitates the insects in the water.

- **Carp**

Carp are bottom-dwelling fish caught using dough balls or corn as bait. Fish in areas with ***shallow, weedy water*** and wait for the carp to come to the surface to feed.

Cast your bait near the weeds and retrieve it slowly and steadily. When you feel a bite, wait a few seconds before setting the hook to ensure the carp has fully taken the bait. Remember that carp are likely forceful and may put up a good fight, so use strong tackle and be patient when reeling them in.

It's essential to research the techniques and baits that work best for each species of fish you are targeting and to be patient while waiting for a bite.

Gear and Equipment for Bank Fishing

Bank fishing is an enjoyable activity that requires a few essential items to ensure a safe and successful fishing experience.

Here are some crucial pieces of gear and equipment you'll need:

✓ **Fishing Rod and Reel**

Select a fishing rod and reel appropriate for your target fish.

A light to medium-action spinning rod and reel is perfect for panfish and trout, while a heavier baitcasting rod and reel may be more suitable for bass and catfish.

✓ Fishing Line and Terminal Tackle

You'll also need a fishing line and terminal tackle such as hooks, weights, and lures or bait. A tackle box or fishing backpack can help keep your gear organized and easily accessible.

✓ Other Important Items

A landing net is an essential tool to land and release fish safely. *A pair of pliers* will help you remove hooks, while *a fish-friendly mat* can protect the fish while removing hooks or taking photos. *A sturdy and comfortable folding chair* can also make bank fishing more enjoyable. Also, do not forget to bring *sunscreen, insect repellent, and a hat* to protect yourself from the sun.

Techniques for Bank Fishing

Bank fishing is likely a rewarding experience with a bit of know-how.

Here are some techniques to keep in mind to improve your chances of success:

✓ **Locating Fish**

Start by locating the fish by reading the water and ***looking for signs of fish activity*** such as surface disturbances, jumping fish, or feeding birds.

Also,

Try to fish in areas with underwater structures or vegetation where fish may be hiding or feeding.

✓ **Using the Appropriate Bait or Lures**

Using the appropriate bait or lures for the species of fish you are targeting is crucial.

Therefore,

Experiment with different baits and techniques until you find what works best. This may involve using live bait, such as worms or lures that mimic the fish's natural prey.

- ✓ **Patience is Key**

Be patient, as it may take some time to get a bite. Be prepared to spend some time in one spot and wait for the fish to come to you.

And as you wait,

Try different casting distances and retrieve speeds to see what attracts the fish.

- ✓ **Awareness of Weather and Water Conditions**

Be aware of the weather and water conditions, as these can affect fish behavior. ***Fish may be more active during*** cloudy or overcast days or low-light conditions in the early morning or late evening.

- ✓ **Practice Good Catch-and-Release Techniques**

Finally, always practice good catch-and-release techniques to ensure the fish population remains healthy and sustainable for future generations. Handle the fish gently and release them quickly to minimize stress and injury.

Having understood the different types of fishing, let's move on to the next chapter and learn about techniques for successful fishing.

SECTION THREE: TECHNIQUES FOR SUCCESSFUL FISHING

Whether just starting or looking to sharpen your skills, mastering the proper techniques is crucial to becoming a successful angler. While having the right gear and equipment is important, it's equally essential to know the right strategies, such as reading the weather, water, and fish behavior and using lures effectively.

In this section, we'll cover everything you need to know to improve your fishing game and ensure you always go home with a big catch.

Let's dive right in!

Chapter Thirteen: Understanding Fish Behavior, Anatomy, and Habitats

Understanding fish behavior, anatomy, and habits is essential for becoming a successful and knowledgeable angler.

Why?

- ✓ By learning about these critical aspects of fish, you can better predict where and when they'll feed, and what type of bait or lure they will likely go after.

- ✓ You'll also be able to determine the best fishing techniques and strategies for a particular fish species. For example, some fish feed close to the surface while others prefer to stay close to the bottom, so knowing these habits can help you choose the right bait and lure and fish at the correct depth.

- ✓ Additionally, understanding fish anatomy can help you to hook and land fish more effectively by knowing where to aim your cast and how to set the hook.

By mastering these skills, you'll be well on your way to becoming a pro angler and reeling in your fair share of fish.

That said, let's take a deeper look at the anatomy of fish and how understanding it can help you fish more successfully.

- **The Anatomy of Fish**

To understand the anatomy of fish, you have to understand the different body parts of fish and their senses to know how fish navigate and survive in water.

The Body Parts of Fish

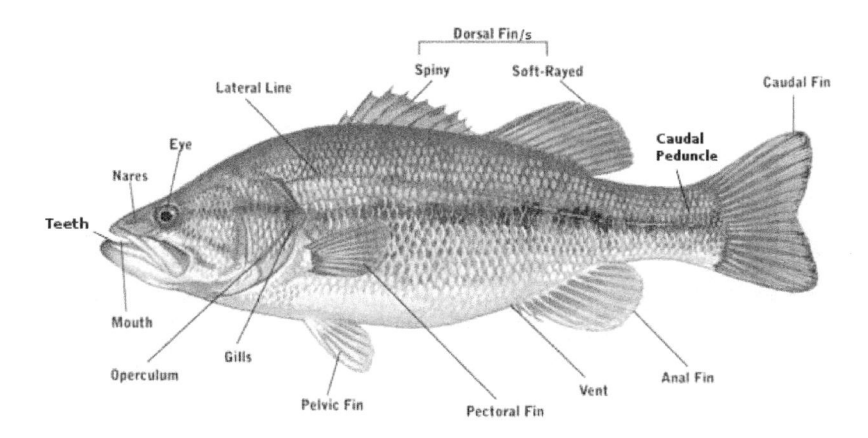

Here are the different body parts of fish:

✓ *Fins*

When you're fishing, understanding ***the different types of fins*** can help you determine how a fish moves through the water.

Here are the types of fins in a fish:

1. **The dorsal fin** helps the fish maintain stability, especially when swimming straight

2. **The pectoral fins** on both sides of the fish's body aid in turning and stopping, providing maneuverability.

3. **The caudal fin, or tail**, is the primary fin that propels the fish through the water. The shape of the caudal fin can also give you an idea of how fast the fish can swim.

Knowing about **the shape of a fish's fins** can help you as a fisherman because it provides valuable insights into the fish's behavior and movement in the water, ultimately leading to more successful fishing.

For example, some fish have **triangular-shaped fins**, which indicate that they are fast swimmers and prefer to move quickly through the water. Knowing this, you may choose to use a speedier retrieval speed or a bait that mimics the movements of a fast-swimming fish to attract these types of fish.

On the other hand, some fish have **longer, more slender fins**, which indicates that they are slower swimmers and prefer to move more delicately through the water. In this case, you may want to use a slower retrieval speed or a more subtle bait presentation to attract these types of fish.

Additionally,

The position and movement of a fish's fins can also provide clues about its behavior. For example, seeing a fish with ***its dorsal fin raised*** may signify aggression or territoriality. Alternatively, suppose you notice a fish with ***its pectoral fins flared out***. In that case, it may suggest it's trying to maintain its position in the water or stabilize itself against the current.

By paying attention to the shape, position, and movement of a fish's fins, you can better understand their behavior and tailor your fishing approach accordingly, ultimately leading to more successful fishing.

1) Scales

As a beginner angler, you should know that fish scales protect the fish from predators and reduce friction as the fish moves through the water.

The size and shape of scales can vary depending on the fish species. For example, fish that live in fast-moving water may have tiny, more streamlined scales that allow them to move more quickly.

2) Gills

Fish breathe through gills, which extract oxygen from the water.

Understanding ***the location and size of the gills*** can help you determine where to place your bait or lure for the optimal catch. For example, if you're fishing for a species that feeds near the surface, you may want to cast your bait or lure shallower to entice the fish to bite.

3) Mouth

The size and shape of a fish's mouth can give you a clue about its diet and feeding behavior.

For example, fish with small mouths, such as trout, are often insectivores, while fish with larger mouths, such as bass, may prey on smaller fish. Knowing the type of food a fish eats can help you select the appropriate bait or lure.

4) Eyes

Fish eyes are adapted to underwater vision, and ***the size and position*** of the eyes can indicate a fish's feeding habits.

For example,

Fish with eyes on the sides of their head, such as flounder, are often bottom-dwellers and have a diet of crustaceans and other bottom-dwelling creatures. Fish with eyes on the front of their head, such as predatory fish like bass and pike, have a diet of smaller fish and have a hunting behavior.

5) Lateral line

The lateral line is a sensory organ that runs along the side of a fish's body. It helps the fish detect changes in water pressure, movement, and vibrations.

Understanding how the lateral line works can help you select lures and bait that imitate prey movements and attract fish. For example, lures that vibrate or disturb the water can trigger the lateral line and attract fish to your bait.

- ## Understanding Fish Habitats, Behavior Patterns, and Tendencies

Understanding fish habitats, behavior patterns, and tendencies is something you have to do if you want to improve your chances of success on the water.

Here are tips to help you become a better angler by understanding fish behavior:

1) Identify Preferred Habitats

Various species of fish have different habitat preferences. For example, largemouth bass prefers shallow, weedy areas, while trout prefer cold, clear waters with plenty of cover. By identifying the preferred habitat of your target species, you can increase your chances of catching them.

Here is a list of different fish species and their preferred habitats:

Fish Species	Preferred Habitats
Rainbow Trout	Cold, clear streams and lakes with gravel bottoms
Largemouth Bass	Warm, quiet waters with cover such as lily pads, logs, and weed beds
Bluegill	Shallow, weedy areas with warm water
Northern Pike	Clear, weedy lakes or slow-moving rivers with cool water
Channel Catfish	Rivers and streams with sandy or rocky bottoms
Walleye	Deep, clear lakes with rocky or gravel bottoms
Brown Trout	Cold, clear streams and rivers with rocky bottoms
Musky	Large, clear lakes and rivers with deep water and abundant cover

Crappie	Clear, weedy lakes or slow-moving rivers with warm water
Yellow Perch	Clear, shallow lakes with sandy or muddy bottoms

2) Study Feeding Patterns

Fish have different feeding patterns depending on their species, size, and location. Some species, like carp, feed primarily on the bottom, while others, like topwater predators, feed on surface-dwelling prey.

Understanding the feeding patterns of the fish you're targeting can help you select the right bait or lure.

Below is a table to illustrate different fish species and their feeding patterns:

Fish Species	**Feeding Patterns**
Rainbow Trout	Opportunistic feeder, feeding on aquatic insects, crustaceans, and small fish
Largemouth Bass	Ambush predator, feeding on small fish, crayfish, frogs, and

	insects
Bluegill	Omnivorous feeder, feeding on insects, small fish, and plant matter
Northern Pike	Ambush predator, feeding on smaller fish, crayfish, frogs, and even small mammals
Channel Catfish	Bottom feeder, feeding on insects, crustaceans, and small fish
Walleye	Nighttime predator, feeding on small fish, crayfish, and insects
Brown Trout	Opportunistic feeder, feeding on insects, small fish, and crustaceans
Musky	Ambush predator, feeding on smaller fish and other aquatic creatures such as crayfish
Crappie	Feeds primarily on small fish and aquatic insects

Yellow Perch	Feeds on small fish, insects, and plankton

3) Learn Seasonal Patterns

Fish behavior can vary seasonally, with different species exhibiting various patterns throughout the year. For example, in the spring, largemouth bass tends to spawn in shallow waters, while in the fall, they move to deeper areas in preparation for winter.

Below is a table to illustrate the behavior of different species in different seasons:

Fish Species	**Seasonal Patterns**
Rainbow Trout	In the spring, they spawn in shallow gravel beds and feed on insects; in the summer, they move to cooler, deeper waters. In the fall, they eat heavily in preparation for winter.
Largemouth Bass	In the spring, they spawn in shallow waters with cover; in

	the summer, they move to deeper, cooler waters with cover. In the fall, they feed heavily in preparation for winter.
Bluegill	In the spring and summer, they spawn in shallow, weedy areas and feed on insects. In the fall, they move to deeper waters and feed on plankton.
Northern Pike	In the spring, they spawn in shallow weedy bays and feed heavily; in the summer, they move to deeper, cooler waters with cover. In the fall, they consume heavily in preparation for winter.
Channel Catfish	In the spring and summer, they spawn in shallow, warm waters and feed heavily. In the fall, they move to deeper waters and rely on baitfish for food.

Walleye	In the spring, they spawn in shallow, rocky areas and feed heavily; in the summer, they move to deeper waters with structure. In the fall, they eat heavily in preparation for winter.
Brown Trout	In the spring, they spawn in shallow gravel beds and feed on insects; in the summer, they move to cooler, deeper waters. In the fall, they consume heavily in preparation for winter.
Musky	In the spring, they spawn in shallow, weedy areas and feed heavily; in the summer, they move to deeper waters with cover. In the fall, they feed heavily in preparation for winter.
Crappie	In the spring, they spawn in shallow waters with cover and

	feed heavily; in the summer, they move to deeper, cooler waters with structure. In the fall, they feed heavily in preparation for winter.
Yellow Perch	In the spring and summer, they spawn in shallow, weedy areas and feed on insects. In the fall, they move to deeper waters and feed on plankton.

By understanding seasonal patterns, you can target the right areas and use the right baits or lures for the time of year.

4) Identify Hiding Spots

Many fish, especially predators, hide in cover to ambush their prey. You can increase your chances of catching fish by identifying these hiding spots, such as fallen trees, rock formations, or weed beds. For example, northern pike lurks in weed beds, waiting to ambush unsuspecting prey.

Here is a table illustrating different fish species and their preferred hiding spots:

Fish Species	Hiding Spots
Largemouth Bass	Underwater structures such as fallen trees, weed beds, and rocks
Rainbow Trout	Behind rocks, in deep pools, and under overhanging vegetation
Walleye	Near rocky structures, drop-offs, and weed lines
Northern Pike	Weed beds, fallen trees, and other submerged vegetation
Catfish	Near underwater structures such as logs, stumps, and rock piles
Crappie	Near brush piles, weed beds, and submerged timber
Bluegill	Near weed beds, logs, and other underwater structures

Musky	Near rocky structures, weed beds, and other underwater covers
Carp	Near the bottom in shallow areas, particularly around aquatic vegetation
Smallmouth Bass	Near rocky structures, drop-offs, and submerged logs

5) Pay Attention to the Water Depth

Fish are sensitive to changes in water depth, and different species have different depth preferences. For example, smallmouth bass tends to prefer deeper waters than largemouth bass. By understanding the depth preferences of your target species, you can adjust your fishing strategy accordingly.

Here are different fish species and their preferred water depths:

Fish Species	Water Depth
Largemouth Bass	1-6 feet
Rainbow Trout	1-5 feet
Walleye	15-30 feet
Northern Pike	3-10 feet
Catfish	Varies, often found near the bottom
Crappie	10-20 feet
Bluegill	3-6 feet
Musky	10-20 feet
Carp	Near the bottom in shallow areas
Smallmouth Bass	5-15 feet

You can become a more successful angler by understanding fish habitats, behavior patterns, and tendencies. Take the time to learn about the fish species you're targeting and the environment you're fishing in, and adjust your strategy accordingly. With patience, persistence, and a bit of knowledge, you'll be reeling in fish in no time.

Let's move on to the next chapter and further perfect our fishing techniques.

Chapter Fourteen: Reading the Water and Finding Fish

Did you know that water contains various information, such as the depth, temperature, and structure of the environment, which can help you determine where the fish are likely to be located?

Well, now you know!

By understanding these factors, you can decide which lures to use, how to retrieve them, and where to cast your line. Additionally, reading the water can help you anticipate changes in the environment, such as incoming storms or changing tides, which can also impact fish behavior.

Without this skill, you may waste valuable time and resources casting your line in areas unlikely to yield a catch.

Therefore,

Learning to read the water is crucial to successful fishing and can significantly increase your chances of landing a big one.

How to Identify that There is Fish in an Area

Here are nine signs you should look out for to know that there are fish in a particular area or point in the water:

1. Ripple or Disturbance on the Water Surface

Keep an eye out for any ripples or disturbances on the water surface, as it may indicate that fish are actively feeding or swimming around. These disturbances are caused by fish jumping, chasing after prey, or swimming near the surface.

2. Bird Activity

Watch out for birds, particularly those that feed on fish like seagulls, cormorants, and herons. Seeing birds diving into the water or circling a specific area may indicate the presence of fish.

3. Currents and Eddies

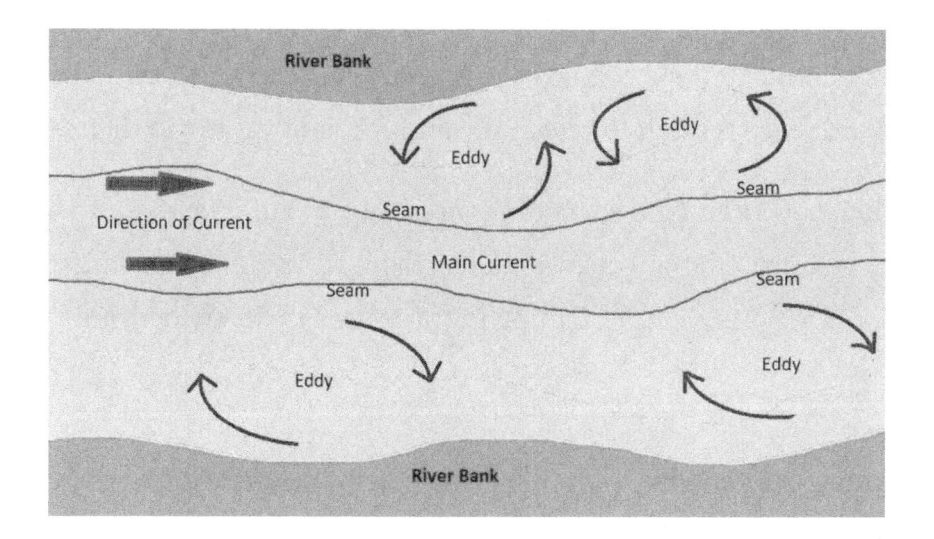

Water currents and eddies can play a significant role in identifying where you can find fish bodies of water. **Currents are** the continuous flow of water in a particular direction. E**ddies are** circular currents or whirlpools that form when water moves around obstructions or changes in the water's depth. These movements in the water can create turbulence, bringing food sources to the surface or concentrating them in a specific area, attracting fish.

Fish tend to gather in areas with a concentration of food or where they can shelter from the current's force.

For example, **when a current hit a large rock or boulder**, the water may slow down, creating a pocket of slower-moving water behind it. This scenario can create an eddy, which is an excellent place for fish to rest and wait for food to come to them.

Similarly, **where two currents meet**, they can create an area of turbulence that attracts smaller fish, which attracts larger predator fish. As a result, fishing in these areas is likely fruitful.

So,

How do you know that a place has currents and eddies?

One way to identify areas with currents and eddies is to **look for changes in water movement or direction**. For example, if you notice the water moving differently or see an area of slower-moving water, it could indicate an eddy or a pocket of food concentration that may attract fish.

4. Underwater Vegetation

Fish are attracted to underwater vegetation, as it provides them with shelter and a food source. Look out for areas with much greenery, particularly submerged ones, as they may be a good spot for fish to congregate.

Here is a table to illustrate different fish species and the kind of vegetation they are attracted to:

Fish Species	The Underwater Vegetation they Prefer
Largemouth Bass	Submerged vegetation such as hydrilla and milfoil
Bluegill	Lily pads, weed beds, and other submerged or floating vegetation
Northern Pike	Weed beds, lily pads, and other submerged or floating vegetation
Carp	Aquatic plants such as duckweed, water lilies, and pondweeds
Rainbow Trout	Areas with fast-moving, oxygenated water near submerged logs or boulders
Walleye	Rocky areas with submerged vegetation or weed beds
Smallmouth Bass	Rock piles, boulder fields, and areas with submerged vegetation

Catfish	Sunken logs, brush piles, and other structures near the bottom
Crappie	Submerged brush piles, stumps, and other structures near the bottom
Musky	Weed beds, rocky areas, and other structures near the bottom or mid-depths

5. Temperature Changes

Fish are sensitive to changes in water temperature and tend to gather in areas where the water is ***slightly warmer or colder than the surrounding water***.

Use ***a thermometer*** to check the water temperature in different locations and look for any temperature changes that may indicate the presence of fish.

6. Shadows and Reflections

Look for shadows or reflections on the water's surface, which may indicate the presence of fish swimming near the surface or bottom.

7. Bubbles

Watch out for bubbles rising to the surface, particularly in shallow water. This sign may indicate the presence of fish or other aquatic life, as they may be stirring up sediment or feeding near the bottom.

8. Previous Catch

If you or someone else has caught fish in a specific area before, it may be a good indication that fish are still in that area.

9. Sonar or Fish Finder

If you have access to a sonar or fish finder device, it can help you locate fish by showing you their position and depth in the water.

Remember, these are just some of the signs to look out for, and there may be other indicators depending on the type of fish you are trying to catch and the body of water you are fishing in. Keep a keen eye out and pay attention to any environmental changes to increase your chances of catching fish.

Let's move on to the next chapter and learn the strategies you can use to fish in different weather conditions.

Chapter Fifteen: Strategies for Fishing in Different Weather Conditions

While some people prefer to fish on a sunny day, others prefer to do so on a chilly and cloudy day.

However,

To be a pro at fishing, you'll need to learn the strategies for fishing in different weather conditions. That way, you'll always catch fish no matter what the weather looks like. After all, the day could start as sunny, only for the rain to pour at noon when you are fishing. In such a case, you must change your fishing strategies to match the current weather.

That said, let's look at the methods you can use to fish in different weather conditions:

Tips on How to Find and Catch Fish in Different Weather Conditions

1. Sunny Weather

During sunny weather, fish may seek shelter in **deeper water or undercover.** You can look for areas with underwater structures, such as drop-offs, ledges, or hollow logs, as these can provide cover and shade for fish. Additionally, you can look for areas with vegetation, such as weed beds, as these can give fish shelter.

And which techniques are ideal for sunny weather?

To catch fish in this condition, you can use techniques such as ***jigging or drop-shotting*** with bait that can mimic the movement of prey, as fish will be more likely to strike something that looks like their usual food source. You can also try using ***lighter-colored bait or lures***, as they may be more visible to fish in the bright sunlight.

2. Cloudy or Overcast Conditions

When it is cloudy, you can try using ***topwater baits***, such as poppers or buzz baits, as they create a commotion on the surface that can attract fish. Additionally, ***darker-colored bait or lures*** are likely more effective in overcast conditions, standing out against the cloudy sky.

3. Windy Conditions

Windy conditions can cause baitfish to move around, attracting larger predator fish. You can look for **areas where the wind blows into** the shore or near underwater structures, creating a concentration of baitfish. Additionally, you can try fishing **near cover areas**, such as rocks or vegetation, where fish may seek shelter from the wind.

You can use baits or lures that mimic the movement of baitfish, such as swimbaits or crankbaits.

4. Rainy Weather

During rainy weather, fish may be more active and feed on baitfish washed into the water. You can look for **areas where runoff enters the body of water**, such as inlets or streams, as this can create a concentration of baitfish. Additionally, you can look for **areas with underwater structures**, such as drop-offs or ledges, as these can provide cover for fish.

During rainy weather, you can use baits or lures that imitate the movement of worms or other bottom-dwelling creatures, as the rain can wash them into the water. Additionally, you may want to try fishing in **shallower waters** or near areas where runoff enters the body of water, as this can create a concentration of baitfish.

5. Cold Weather

During colder weather, fish may be more sluggish and less active. You can look for **areas where the water is warmer**, such as near power plant outflows or shallow regions that receive more sunlight. Additionally, you can look for **areas with underwater structures**, such as deep pools or rock ledges, as these can provide cover for fish seeking warmer water.

To catch fish in this condition, you can try using bait that is smaller and moves slower, such as jigs or live bait. You may also want to try fishing near areas where the water is warmer, such as near power plant outflows or shallow regions, as they receive more sunlight.

Now that you know how to fish in different weather conditions, what should you do when you apply these techniques but the fish aren't biting on the bait?

Let's find out in the next chapter.

Chapter Sixteen: When Fish Aren't Biting; What Do You Do?

Fishing is rewarding and exciting, but what happens when you've spent hours on the water and the fish aren't biting?

It's frustrating and can leave even the most experienced angler feeling defeated. But fear not! This chapter is dedicated to helping you navigate those frustrating moments when the fish won't seem to cooperate.

To be precise,

We'll explore different strategies and techniques to help you increase your chances of catching fish, even when the conditions aren't in your favor. So buckle up and get ready to learn some tips and tricks to help you turn those slow days on the water into a success!

But first, let's understand the problem:

1. Why Fish May Not Be Biting

Here are some reasons why fish may not be biting:

- **Water Temperature**

Fish are cold-blooded, meaning their body temperature matches the surrounding water. Their metabolism and activity levels are affected by water temperature, so if the water is too cold or too warm, fish may not be as active and may not be interested in feeding.

For example, coldwater fish like trout may be less active in warm water, while warm-water fish like bass may be less active in cold water.

- **Water Clarity**

Fish rely on their vision to locate prey, so if the water is murky or dirty, it can make it more difficult to see and find food. Rain, wind, and water runoff contribute to reduced water clarity.

In some cases, fish may be able to adjust to these conditions by relying more on their ***sense of smell or lateral line*** (a sensory system that detects vibrations in the water). However, this can make catching them using traditional fishing methods more difficult.

- **Barometric Pressure**

Changes in barometric pressure can affect fish behavior and feeding patterns. **When the barometric pressure drops** (often associated with an approaching storm), it can cause fish to become less active and ***less likely to feed***.

Some anglers believe that falling pressure can trigger a feeding frenzy in some species, but this is not always true.

- **Time of Day**

Some fish are more active and feed more during certain times of the day. For example, some fish species may feed more at dawn or dusk when the light is low and their prey is more active. Other species may feed more during the middle of the day when the sun is high, and the water is warmer.

Here is a table to illustrate different fish species and the best time to fish them:

Fish Species	Best Time to Fish
Rainbow Trout	Early morning or late afternoon
Largemouth Bass	Early morning or late evening
Smallmouth Bass	Early morning or late

	afternoon
Walleye	Late evening or early morning
Northern Pike	Early morning or late afternoon
Catfish	Evening or night
Crappie	Early morning or late afternoon
Bluegill	Morning or evening
Musky	Early morning or late afternoon
Carp	Morning or evening

- **Water Depth**

Different fish species prefer different water depths, and if you're not fishing in the correct depth, you may not be targeting the suitable species. Some fish may be found in shallow water near the shore, while others like deeper water offshore.

Factors like water temperature, clarity, and time of day can influence where fish are likely to be found.

- **Fishing Pressure**

If an area has been heavily fished or there are many boats and anglers in the water, it can make fish more cautious and less likely to bite.

Sometimes, fish may become "educated" and learn to avoid specific lures or bait. This is why it's essential to practice catch-and-release fishing and to prevent overfishing in popular fishing areas.

2. The Solutions: How to Change Fishing Techniques and Make Fish Bite

To make fish bite, you must first understand why they are not biting. That way, you'll be able to adjust your fishing techniques accordingly.

That said, let's look at the solution for each of the causes discussed above:

- **Measure the Water Temperature**

If you discover that the fish aren't biting because of the water temperature, use a thermometer to measure the water temperature and target species known to be active in those conditions.

Slow down your retrieval speed in colder water and use smaller lures or bait. Try fishing deeper or using topwater lures in warmer water early in the morning or late in the evening.

- **Use Attractive Lures**

To help fish bite even when the water isn't clear, you can use lures or bait that create more vibration or scent to attract fish in murky water.

Alternatively, switch to fishing in areas with clearer water, such as near the mouth of a creek or river.

- **Use Lures that Complement the Barometric Pressure**

It is advisable to fish during stable weather conditions when the barometric pressure is consistent.

However, if you must fish during changing conditions, try using slow-moving lures or bait that mimic injured prey to entice fish that may be less active.

- **Choose the Right Time of Day**

Research the feeding habits of your target species and fish during their preferred feeding times. Alternatively, try fishing in deeper water during the hottest part of the day or near the surface during low-light conditions.

- **Adjust Fishing Depth**

Adjust your fishing depth based on the species you are targeting and the conditions of the water. Use a fishfinder or depth chart to locate fish at the correct depth and try different techniques like jigging or trolling to cover more water.

- **Be Ware of Seasonal Patterns**

Research the seasonal patterns of your target species and adjust your fishing techniques accordingly. For example, use lures or bait that mimic the prey that fish feed during that time of year.

- **Be Unpredictable to Make Even the Most Cautious Fish Bite**

If the fish refuses to bite because they are suspicious and hence more cautious, try fishing in less crowded areas or during less popular times of the day. Use lures or bait less commonly used in that area or switch to a different fishing technique altogether.

Remember to practice catch-and-release fishing to help maintain healthy fish populations.

3. How to Adjust Baits and Lures to Encourage Fish to Bite

You can also play around with baits and lures in the following ways to encourage fish to bite:

- **Change the Color**

Sometimes, a color change could be all it takes to entice a fish to bite. If you've been using a bright lure or bait, try switching to a more natural color or a different hue contrasting with the water.

- **Vary the Retrieve Speed**

Fish may not be interested in a lure or bait that moves too quickly or slowly. Experiment with different retrieval speeds to find the sweet spot that entices fish to bite.

- **Add Scent**

Adding scent to your lure or bait can make it more attractive to fish. You can use artificial odors or natural scents like live bait or fish oil to create a trail that draws fish toward your bait.

- **Change the Size or Shape**

Sometimes, a change in size or shape can make all the difference. If you've used a large lure or bait and didn't catch anything, try downsizing to something smaller. Alternatively, try using a different type of lure or bait with a different shape or profile.

- **Adjust the Depth**

Fish may be more active at different depths depending on the time of day and weather conditions. Adjust the depth of your bait or lure to find where the fish feed. You can use a fish finder or depth chart to help you locate fish at the correct depth.

- **Change the Action**

Various lures and baits have different actions that can mimic the movement of prey. Experiment with multiple acts like a jerky or steady retrieve with pauses to see what triggers fish to bite.

- **Use a Trailer Hook**

Add a trailer hook if fish are striking your bait or lure but not getting hooked. Doing this can increase your chances of catching fish that are striking short.

Summary: When adjusting baits and lures to encourage fish to bite, paying attention to the fish's conditions and behavior is essential. Be patient and experiment with different techniques until you find the best for your target species.

Hopefully, you are gaining as much knowledge as you need to be a pro at fishing.

Let's move on to the next section and learn even more tips.

SECTION FOUR: CATCHING AND HANDLING FISH

After spending hours on the water, there's nothing quite like the thrill of finally reeling in a fish. Whether you're an experienced angler or a novice fisherman, a sense of excitement and accomplishment comes with catching your dinner.

But,

The process doesn't stop there.

Once you've hooked a fish, you must know how to handle it properly to ensure it stays healthy and safe for consumption.

In this section, we'll explore the essential techniques for catching and handling fish, from when you feel a tug on your line to when you prepare it for cooking.

So grab your fishing gear, and let's dive in!

Chapter Seventeen: Proper Handling of Fish

Before we even go into how to handle fish properly, why is it essential in the first place?

The Importance of Catching and Handling Fish Properly

Here are a few reasons why you need to handle your fish properly:

1. Ensures Health and safety

Proper fish handling after catching is crucial for reducing the risk of foodborne illness. Fish can carry **harmful bacteria** such as E. coli, Salmonella, and Listeria, as well as **parasites** that can cause serious health problems if consumed.

The risk of illness is significantly reduced by handling fish carefully, keeping it clean and cold, and cooking it to the appropriate temperature.

2. Preserves Fish Quality

Proper fish handling can help maintain its flavor and texture, making it a more enjoyable meal. For example, stress during the catch and release process can cause the fish to produce **_lactic acid_**, affecting the meat's taste and texture.

Minimizing stress on the fish and cooling it immediately after catching it can preserve the quality of the meat. Also, properly storing and handling the fish after capturing can help prevent spoilage and maintain freshness.

3. Promotes Sustainable Fishing Practices

Proper handling of fish after catching can promote sustainable fishing practices. Catch-and-release fishing, for example, can effectively preserve fish populations, but only if the fish are handled carefully and released unharmed.

By using barbless hooks, gently handling the fish, and quickly releasing it back into the water, anglers can help ensure that the fish survive and continue to breed and contribute to the population.

4. Respects the Environment

Proper handling of fish after catching also respects the environment. By avoiding unnecessary harm to fish and their habitats, anglers can help protect the delicate balance of ecosystems.

Properly disposing of fishing waste, such as lines, hooks, and bait, also helps prevent harm to wildlife and their habitats.

By practicing responsible fishing, anglers can help preserve the environment for future generations.

The Ethics of Fishing: Balancing Enjoyment and Responsibility

Here is how you will be ethical even as you enjoy fishing:

- **Practice Catch-and-Release Fishing**

Catch-and-release fishing is a great way to enjoy fishing while being responsible and respectful of fish populations.

By releasing fish back into the water unharmed, anglers can help ensure that fish populations remain healthy and sustainable. When practicing catch-and-release fishing, handling the fish gently, using barbless hooks, and quickly releasing the fish are essential to remember.

- **Follow Fishing Regulations**

Fishing regulations are in place to protect fish populations and ensure sustainable fishing practices.

Therefore,

Following these regulations, such as catch limits, size limits, and closed seasons, is essential to help preserve fish populations and respect the environment.

What if you don't?

Ignoring fishing regulations can have serious consequences, including fines and damage to fish populations.

- **Use Ethical Fishing Gear**

Some fishing gear can cause unnecessary harm to fish, such as ***gill nets and certain types of hooks***. It's important to use ethical fishing gear, such as circle hooks and fish-friendly nets, to minimize harm to fish populations.

Using ethical fishing gear allows anglers to enjoy fishing while being responsible and respectful.

- **Respect the Environment**

Fishing is a great way to enjoy nature and the environment, but it's essential to do so responsibly.

What does this mean?

✓ You respect the habitats of fish and other wildlife

✓ You properly dispose of fishing waste

- ✓ You avoid damage to sensitive ecosystems

By respecting the environment, anglers can help preserve it for future generations.

- **Practice Proper Fish Handling and Care**

Proper fish handling and care are essential for ensuring the health and safety of both fish and humans. This includes using appropriate fishing techniques, minimizing stress on fish during catch-and-release fishing, and properly cleaning and preparing fish for consumption.

Again, by practicing proper fish handling and care, anglers can enjoy fishing while being responsible and respectful.

Let's move on to the next chapter and learn about the fish you should not fish.

Chapter Eighteen: Fish Not to Fish

As an angler, getting excited about catching various fish is easy. However, it's important to remember that ***not all fish are suitable for catching and consumption.***

In fact,

There are several types of fish you or any other angler should not fish due to concerns about overfishing, population depletion, and environmental impact.

In this chapter, we'll explore some fish that should not be fished and learn why. From endangered species to toxic fish, understanding why you should avoid these fish is essential for responsible fishing and preserving fish populations for future generations.

So, please put down your fishing rod and join us as we dive into the world of 'the fish not to fish.'

- **Protecting Endangered Species**

Endangered fish species are those that are at ***risk of becoming extinct***. This risk is due to several reasons, including overfishing, habitat destruction, pollution, and climate change. As a responsible citizen, it's essential to understand the gravity of the situation and the impact that our actions can have on endangered fish populations.

Fishing endangered fish species can severely affect the individual fish and the overall population.

Here is how:

- ✓ When a species is already endangered, any additional stressor, such as fishing, can significantly impact its ability to recover.

- ✓ Catching endangered fish species can also injure or kill the individual fish, especially if caught using unsustainable fishing practices or gear.

- ✓ Furthermore, fishing endangered fish species can contribute to the overall depletion of the species, further increasing their risk of extinction. This can have severe consequences for the entire ecosystem, as these fish play essential roles in maintaining the balance and health of aquatic ecosystems. For example, some endangered fish species are important predators that help control the populations of other species, while others are critical prey species for larger predators. Losing these species can have cascading effects throughout the ecosystem, impacting everything from water quality to the viability of other species.

Ultimately, fishing endangered fish species can have long-lasting and far-reaching consequences, making it crucial to avoid targeting them and support conservation efforts to protect them.

Endangered Fish Species That are Illegal to Fish in Certain Areas

Here are examples of fish species that are illegal to catch in specific areas:

1. Atlantic Bluefin Tuna

This highly prized fish has been severely overfished, leading to a decline in population.

Fishing Atlantic bluefin tuna in some areas, including **the Mediterranean Sea and the Gulf of Mexico**, is illegal.

2. Pacific Bluefin Tuna

Similar to its Atlantic counterpart, the Pacific bluefin tuna has been heavily overfished, leading to concerns about its population.

Fishing Pacific bluefin tuna in some areas, including the **Western and Central Pacific Oceans,** is illegal.

3. Chinook Salmon

This iconic fish is an integral part of the Pacific Northwest ecosystem, but its population has been severely impacted by overfishing and habitat loss.

Fishing Chinook salmon in some areas, including **the Columbia River Basin**, is illegal.

4. European Eel

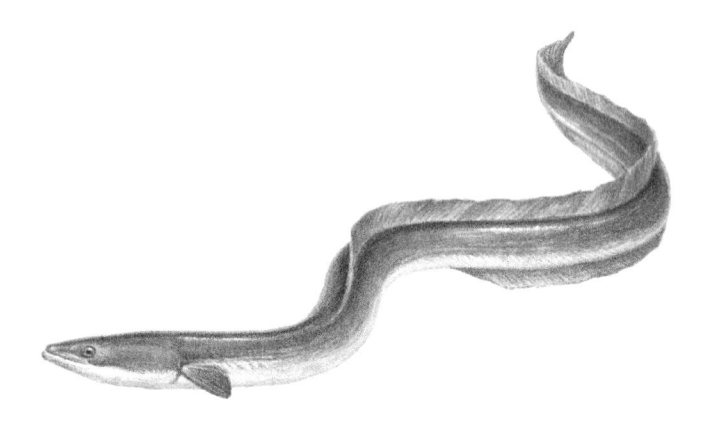

Overfishing, habitat destruction, and other factors have severely impacted this once-common fish.

Fishing European eels in some areas, including the ***European Union***, is illegal.

By avoiding the fishing of these endangered fish species and supporting conservation efforts, we can help protect them and ensure they continue playing a vital role in aquatic ecosystems for generations.

- **The Impact of Overfishing**

You see, even if a particular fish species is not endangered, ***it is unethical to overfish any fish in any location.***

Why?

This is because overfishing poses the following threats:

✓ **Depletion of Fish Populations**

Overfishing leads to declining fish populations, which can lead to the ***extinction*** of entire species.

As mentioned earlier, this can significantly impact the aquatic ecosystem, as different fish species play vital roles in maintaining the balance and health of the ecosystem.

✓ **Disruption of the Food Chain**

Overfishing can also disrupt the food chain in the ecosystem.

For example,

When predator fish species are overfished, it can cause the populations of their prey to increase, leading to a decrease in the populations of other species in the ecosystem.

✓ Destruction of Habitats

Overfishing can destroy habitats as fishermen look for new areas to fish. This can ruin sensitive ecosystems, such as coral reefs or seagrass beds, which provide essential fish and marine life habitats.

✓ Loss of Biodiversity

Overfishing can lead to biodiversity loss in the ecosystem, as some fish species become extinct or their populations decline. This loss can have significant consequences for the health and functioning of the ecosystem, as biodiversity is crucial for maintaining the balance and resilience of the ecosystem.

✓ Economic Threats

Overfishing can have significant economic impacts on communities that rely on fishing for their livelihoods.

Here is how:

When fish populations decline, fishermen can no longer catch as many fish, which can result in economic hardship for fishing communities.

✓ Social Threats

Overfishing can also have social impacts, such as losing cultural traditions and fishing practices.

In addition, overfishing can lead to conflicts between different groups, such as commercial fishermen and recreational anglers.

✓ Climate Change

Overfishing can also exacerbate the effects of climate change on the ecosystem.

For example,

Overfishing of predator fish species can lead to an increase in the populations of their prey, which can result in the overgrazing of algae and other vegetation that help to sequester carbon from the atmosphere.

It's crucial to address the problem of overfishing to ensure the long-term sustainability of fish populations and the health of the aquatic ecosystem.

And,

By implementing sustainable fishing practices and supporting conservation efforts, we can help mitigate the impacts of overfishing and ensure that fish populations and the ecosystem remain healthy and resilient.

- # How to Know the Fish Species to Avoid in Your Area

Identifying the fish species you should avoid fishing in your area is likely a challenging task. Still, it's an essential step to help protect endangered fish populations and preserve the health of the aquatic ecosystem.

Here are some tips to help you identify the fish species you should avoid fishing in your area:

✓ **Research Local Regulations**

Check with your local fishing authority to determine which fish species are protected or endangered in your area.

But where are you checking from?

You can find this information in *fishing regulations and conservation policies*.

Following these guidelines is vital to avoid illegal fishing practices that can harm endangered fish populations.

✓ **Look for Species Lists**

Many conservation organizations provide lists of endangered fish species for different regions. These lists are found *online, in local libraries,* or through *local conservation organizations*.

Take the time to research the fish species in your area and learn which ones are endangered or at risk.

✓ Use Identification Guides

Identification guides are a helpful tool to help you recognize different fish species. These guides can help you identify the fish species you should avoid fishing and assist you in practicing sustainable fishing practices.

So,

Look for guides specific to your area, including endangered or protected species information.

✓ Consult with Local Fishermen

Talking to local fishermen is an excellent way to learn which fish species are endangered in your area.

Why?

Experienced fishermen can provide insights into the behavior and habitat of different fish species and help you understand which species to avoid.

- **Fish Not to Eat**

Apart from conserving the environment and protecting endangered species, some fish should not be eaten.

So,

How do you identify them so you don't eat something poisonous?

Well, here is how:

✓ **Check Seafood Guides**

Seafood guides provide information on which fish are safe to eat and which are best to avoid. These guides are typically organized by region and provide up-to-date information on the health and sustainability of different fish species.

Here is a list of seafood guides you can refer to:

- FishWise Seafood Guide (US)

- Gulf of Maine Research Institute Seafood Guide (US)

- Blue Ocean Institute Seafood Guide (US)

- Greenpeace Seafood Red List (international)

- Fair Trade Seafood Guide (international)

- WWF Seafood Guide (international)

- The Safina Center Seafood Program (US)

- South African Sustainable Seafood Initiative (SASSI) (South Africa)

- Sustainable Seafood Coalition (UK)

- Good Fish Foundation Seafood Guide (Netherlands)

✓ **Look for Mercury Levels**

Certain fish species may contain high levels of mercury, which **can harm your health**. Look for information on the mercury levels of different fish species to avoid consuming fish that may have harmful levels of this toxic substance.

The United States Environmental Protection Agency (EPA) has set a reference dose of ***0.1 micrograms of mercury daily for each kg of body weight*** as the maximum safe mercury level exposure.

✓ **Avoid Endangered Species**

Eating endangered fish species can contribute to their decline in population and harm the environment's overall health.

As such, check with your local fishing authority or conservation organizations to identify which fish species are endangered and avoid eating them.

✓ Consider Sustainable Fishing Practices

Some fish species are overfished or caught using unsustainable fishing practices. Avoid eating fish caught using destructive methods, such as ***bottom trawling***. Also, avoid those at risk of overfishing.

✓ Choose Farmed Fish Carefully

Farmed fish are likely more sustainable alternatives to wild-caught fish, but carefully choosing farmed fish is essential.

So,

Look for fish farmed sustainably without using harmful chemicals or practices that harm the environment.

Following these points and being mindful of the fish you eat can help protect your and the environment's health. Remember to check seafood guides, avoid endangered species, and consider sustainable fishing practices when selecting fish to eat.

- **Examples of Fish that Should Not Be Eaten**

Here are a few examples of fish that are not fit for human consumption:

1) Pufferfish

Pufferfish, also known as fugu, is a delicacy in Japan, but it's also one of the most dangerous fish you can eat.

Here is why:

The pufferfish's liver, ovaries, and skin contain **tetrodotoxin**, a deadly toxin, even in small amounts.

In fact,

One pufferfish can contain enough toxins to **kill 30 people**. Despite this, some people still try to eat pufferfish, but it's important to note that only licensed and trained chefs can prepare it in Japan.

Pufferfish are primarily found in Japan, China, and other parts of Asia.

2) Barracuda

Barracuda is a popular game fish, but it's not recommended for eating due to its ***high levels of mercury***.

Mercury is a toxic heavy metal that can cause neurological damage, especially in young children and pregnant women.

Barracuda are mainly found in tropical and subtropical waters worldwide, including the Caribbean, the Gulf of Mexico, and the Indian Ocean.

3) Bluefish

Bluefish is a popular sport fish, but it's not recommended for eating due to its **_high levels of mercury and PCBs_**.

PCBs are industrial chemicals used in the past and can accumulate in the fatty tissues of fish.

Bluefish are likely found in the Atlantic Ocean, from Maine to Florida.

4) Ciguatera Fish

Ciguatera fish poisoning is caused by eating certain reef fish that have accumulated a **toxin produced by algae** growing on coral reefs. The toxin can cause nausea, vomiting, and neurological symptoms and are likely life-threatening in some cases. Ciguatera fish include barracuda, grouper, snapper, and amberjack.

These fish are found in tropical and subtropical waters around the world.

5) Catfish

While catfish is commonly eaten in many parts of the world, it's not recommended due to its **high levels of contaminants like PCBs and dioxins**. These chemicals can cause cancer and other health problems.

Catfish are likely found in North America's, South America's, and Asia's freshwater rivers and lakes.

Remember, you must be aware of what you're eating regarding fish. Some fish may contain high levels of toxins or contaminants, and it's always better to err on the side of caution concerning your health. If you're unsure whether a particular fish is safe to eat, check with local authorities or research beforehand.

Let's move on to the next chapter and learn how to hook and land a catch like a pro.

Chapter Nineteen: Hooking and Landing a Catch

Whether you're a novice angler or an experienced fisherman, knowing how to hook and land a catch is crucial to having a successful and enjoyable fishing trip.

In this chapter, we will cover the proper techniques for setting the hook, tricking the fish and reeling it in, and how to safely land the fish without causing harm to it or yourself.

So, prepare to improve your fishing skills and increase your chances of reeling in that big catch!

How to set the Hook Properly

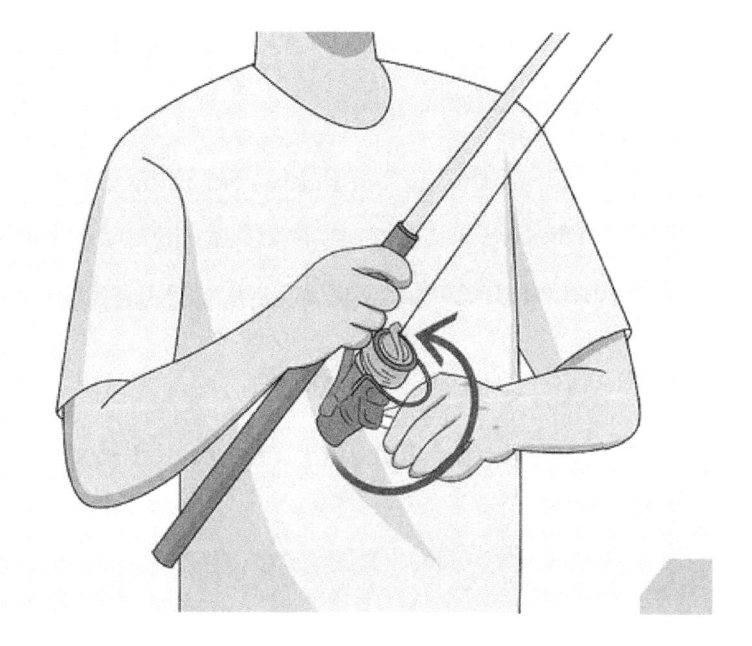

Setting the hook is a crucial part of fishing that many anglers struggle with. It can mean the difference between landing a trophy fish and going home empty-handed.

Follow these steps to set the hook properly and increase your chances of success:

- **Step 1: Wait for the Right Moment**

Before placing the hook, ensure the fish has taken the bait and is hooked.

But how will you know?

You will feel a tug or a pull on the line, and the tip of your fishing rod will likely bend slightly.

- **Step 2: Reel in the Slack**

Once you feel the fish on the line, quickly reel in any slack. This step will help you remove any excess line between you and the fish, giving you more control over the fish when you set the hook.

- **Step 3: Make a Swift, Firm Motion**

When you feel the fish on the line and have reeled in the slack, it's time to set the hook.

How?

Quickly and firmly jerk the rod upwards and back towards you. This motion will lodge the hook deeper into the fish's mouth, increasing your chances of landing it.

- **Step 4: Keep Tension on the Line**

After setting the hook, keep tension on the line by **keeping the rod tip up and reeling in any slack**. Doing this will help prevent the fish from shaking the hook loose and escaping.

- **Step 5: Use the Right Amount of Force**

Using enough force to set the hook is essential, but not so much that you break the line or damage the fish's mouth.

But how will you know the right amount of force?

The amount of force you need will **depend on the size of the fish** and **the type of bait or lure** you are using.

- **Step 6: Be Patient**

Sometimes it takes a few attempts to set the hook properly, especially if the fish is small or not fully committed to falling for the bait.

So,

Don't give up if you miss the first few tries. Keep trying until you feel the hook firmly in the fish's mouth.

By following these steps, you'll be well on setting the hook like a pro and landing more fish on your next fishing trip.

Remember to be patient and keep practicing, as setting the hook is a skill that takes time and experience to master.

How to Play the Fish and Reel it in Like a Pro

After hooking the fish, it is time to bring it out of the water by reeling it in.

Here is how you do it like a pro:

✓ **Keep the Rod's Tip-Up**

Once you have hooked the fish, you want to keep the rod tip up high in the air.

Why?

This position helps prevent the fish from diving and getting tangled in weeds or other underwater debris.

✓ Use the Rod to Tire the Fish Out

When you start reeling in the fish, try to tire it out by pulling the rod back and then reeling in the slack as you lower the rod tip. Repeat this process until the fish is tired and no longer fighting as hard.

✓ Reel in the Slack

Once the fish is tired out, start reeling in the slack line. Be sure to keep the line tight, so the fish cannot shake the hook loose.

✓ Use the Rod to Direct Your Catch

As you reel in the fish, use the rod to direct it away from underwater obstacles or hazards. You can also use the rod to steer the fish toward your landing net.

✓ Keep the Tension On

Throughout the entire process, you want to keep tension on the line. This means keeping the line tight and not letting any slack develop. If the fish can shake the hook loose, it's because there was too much slack in the line.

✓ **Land the Fish**

Once the fish is close enough, scoop it out of the water using a landing net.

So,

If you plan to release the fish, do so quickly and gently. However, be gentle with the fish so as not to injure it.

Let's look at how to land the fish in more detail below.

How to Land the Fish

Congratulations, you've played and reeled in your catch!

Now it's time to land the fish properly to avoid injury to you or the fish.

Here is a step-by-step process of how to do it:

- **Step 1: Get Your Landing Net Ready**

A landing net is designed to help lift the fish out of the water.

When fishing,

Make sure it is correctly assembled and ready to use.

- **Step 2: Position the Fish**

Guide the fish close to you and position it so it's ready to be netted. Keep the fish in the water as much as possible and avoid sudden movements that may startle it.

- **Step 3: Slide the Net under the Fish**

Hold the landing net by the handle and slide it under the fish. During this step, ensure the fish's head is facing into the net and the tail is outside the net.

- **Step 4: Lift the Fish**

Slowly lift the net out of the water, ensuring that the fish is well-supported and not too heavy for the net. Keep the fish in the water as much as possible and avoid sudden movements that may cause it to fall back into the water.

- **Step 5: Remove the Hook**

Once the fish is secure in the net, remove the hook **as quickly and as gently as possible**. Use pliers if necessary, and be careful not to damage the fish's mouth.

- **Step 6: Measure and Weigh the Fish (Optional)**

If you want to measure and weigh the fish, do so while it's still in the net. Use a fish grip or a scale to weigh the fish and a measuring tape to get the length.

- **Step 7: Release or Keep the Fish**

Decide whether to release or keep the fish based on local regulations, size, and species.

If you're releasing the fish, handle it carefully and return it to the water as quickly as possible.

And if you're keeping the fish, put it in a cooler with ice or keep it in the water until you're ready to clean it.

Precautions and Tips when Landing the Fish

- ✓ Use a landing net with a soft mesh to prevent damage to the fish's fins and scales.
- ✓ Keep the fish in the water as much as possible to prevent them from suffocating.

- ✓ Wet your hands before handling the fish to prevent removing the protective slime coat on the fish's skin.

- ✓ Avoid squeezing or putting pressure on the fish's abdomen, as this can damage its internal organs.

- ✓ Use barbless hooks or flatten the barbs to make hook removal more manageable and less harmful to the fish.

- ✓ Keep a pair of pliers handy to help with hook removal.

Note: Landing a fish requires patience, skill, and care. By following these steps and taking the necessary precautions, you can safely land and release or keep your catch.

Let's move on to the next chapter and learn how to handle live fish.

Chapter Twenty: Handling Live Fish

Knowing how to handle a fish properly is vital, especially if you plan on releasing it back into the water. Mishandling a fish can result in **severe injury or even death** for the fish.

In this chapter, you will learn how to properly handle live fish, ensuring its survival after the catch. By following these tips and techniques, you can safely release the fish back into the water, allowing it to continue its life cycle and ensuring the sustainability of the fishery.

So, let's dive in and learn how to handle live fish like a pro!

- **Tips for Handling Live Fish to Avoid Injuries**

Here are ten tips on how to handle live fish after landing them to avoid injuring them:

1. **Wet your Hands**

Before touching the fish, wet your hands to reduce the slime that will come off the fish.

Why?

This slime is vital for the fish's health, and removing it can increase **the risk of infection.**

2. Use a Wet Towel

If you're uncomfortable touching the fish directly, use a wet towel or cloth to handle it. This tip will help you maintain a good grip without harming the fish.

3. Support the Fish's Weight

When lifting the fish, support its weight correctly.

How?

Never hold it by the tail or gills, which can cause serious injuries. Instead, **use both hands to hold** the fish gently.

4. Use Pliers or Hemostats

If the fish has swallowed the hook, you can use pliers or hemostats to remove it.

Note: Avoid pulling the hook out forcefully, as this can cause internal injuries.

5. Remove the Hook Quickly

Remove the hook as quickly as possible if the fish is bleeding or has a deep hook injury.

Why?

The longer the hook stays in the fish, the more damage it can do.

6. Keep the Fish in the Water

If you're releasing the fish, let it stay in the water as much as possible. Doing this will help it breathe properly and reduce stress.

7. Hold the Fish Gently

When holding the fish, avoid squeezing it too hard. This grip can damage its internal organs and cause serious injuries.

8. Avoid Touching the Gills

The gills are exceptionally delicate, and touching them ***can cause serious harm*** to the fish. When removing the hook, do so from the fish's mouth, not the gills.

9. Release the Fish Quickly

If you're releasing the fish, do it quickly and gently. Please don't hold the fish out of the water for too long, as this can lead to suffocation.

10. Use a Landing Net

If you're having trouble landing the fish, use a landing net to help you. This net will reduce the required handling and help avoid injuring the fish.

Remember: Handling live fish is a delicate process that requires patience and care. Following these tips ensures the fish remains healthy and strong, even after being caught.

- # How to Remove the Hook without Injuring the Fish

Removing the hook from a landed fish is likely tricky, especially if you want to return it unharmed into the water.

Here is a step-by-step process to safely and effectively remove the hook:

Step 1: Keep the Fish Wet

Before removing the hook, ensure the fish is in water, either in a net or held gently by the body. Wet hands can help protect the fish's slimy coating, which protects them from disease and parasites.

Keeping the fish wet will also help it breathe properly, especially if you've played it for a long time.

Step 2: Determine the Hook Location

Before removing the hook, please take a moment to assess where it's located. It will be easier to remove if it's in the fish's mouth than in its throat or stomach.

Step 3: Use Pliers to Remove the Hook

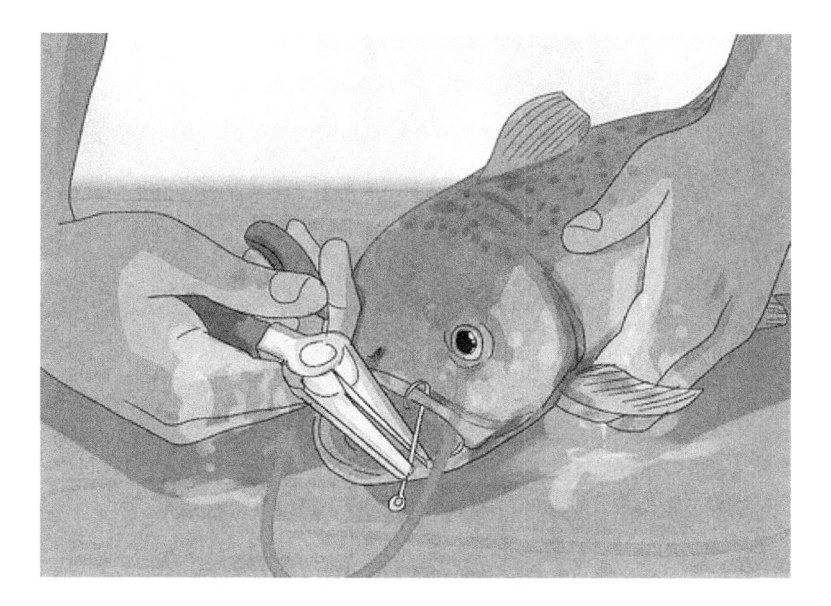

Use pliers to grip the hook's shank, not the pointy end, and gently turn it to release it from the fish's mouth.

Step 4: Remove the Hook Quickly

Once you've determined the hook location, gently (but quickly) remove it from the fish's mouth. Avoid pulling the hook or tugging on it, as this can cause injury to the fish.

Step 5: Cut the Line if Necessary

If the hook is deeply embedded or if you can't remove it quickly, it's better to cut the line as close to the hook as possible and release the fish with the hook still in its mouth. The hook will eventually rust or dissolve, and the fish will heal around it.

Step 6: Don't Squeeze the Fish

When handling the fish, avoid squeezing it, as this can damage its internal organs.

Instead, hold it gently but firmly by the body, supporting its weight with your other hand.

Step 7: Minimize Handling Time

The longer you handle the fish, the more stress it will experience, affecting its chances of survival after release. As such, minimize handling time by quickly removing the hook and returning the fish to the water the soonest as possible.

Step 8: Revive the Fish

If the fish appears lethargic after release, hold it gently in the water, moving it back and forth to encourage water flow over its gills. Doing this will help revive it and ensure it can swim away.

Step 9: Avoid Taking Trophy Shots

While it's tempting to take photos of your catch, doing so can cause harm to the fish. Avoid taking trophy shots unless you have to, and handle the fish gently and briefly if you do.

Step 10: Practice Catch and Release

If you're not planning to eat the fish, consider practicing catch and release. This technique allows the fish to continue growing and reproducing, ensuring a healthy population for years.

The section below will discuss how you catch and release fish back into the waters.

How to Release Fish Back into the Water

Releasing fish back into the water is an integral part of responsible fishing. It helps ensure that fish populations remain healthy and sustainable for future generations.

Here is a step-by-step guide on how to do it properly:

✓ **Prepare your Equipment**

Before releasing the fish, as discussed earlier, ensure you have everything you need, such as pliers or forceps to remove the hook and a net or fish gripper to hold the fish.

✓ **Keep the Fish in the Water**

Try to keep the fish in the water as much as possible. Doing this will help minimize stress and prevent the fish from suffocating.

If possible,

Leave the fish in the net or gripper while preparing to release it.

✓ **Remove the Hook**

Remove the hook with pliers or forceps if the fish is hooked. If the hook is deeply embedded, you may need to cut the line near it and release the fish with the hook still in its mouth. This step will minimize the damage and give the fish a better chance of survival.

✓ **Revive the Fish**

If the fish appears exhausted or disoriented, hold it upright in the water and gently move it back and forth to help oxygenate its gills. Doing this will help revive the fish and increase its chances of survival.

✓ Release the Fish

Once the fish has regained strength, gently release it into the water.

How?

Hold the fish by the tail and gently move it back and forth to help it regain equilibrium.

Note: Avoid throwing or dropping the fish back into the water, which can cause injury or trauma.

✓ Watch the Fish Swim Away

Watch the fish swim away to ensure that it has recovered fully.

If the fish appears to be struggling, you may need to continue to hold it and revive it until it can swim away.

Remember: Properly releasing fish back into the water is essential to being a responsible angler. With these steps, you can help ensure the fish you catch survive and thrive in their natural habitat.

Let's move on to the next chapter and learn about catch and release vs. catch and keep and the pros and cons of each.

Chapter 21: Catch and Release vs. Catch and Keep Practices

The difference between catch-and-release fishing and catch-and-keep fishing is essentially in their name.

Catch-and-release fishing is where you catch fish to release them back into the water unharmed. This method minimizes the impact on fish populations and the ecosystem and preserves the fishing experience for future generations.

On the other hand, ***catch-and-keep fishing*** involves catching fish to keep them to eat or use for other purposes. This fishing method can significantly impact fish populations and the environment, and regulations and restrictions may be in place to manage the number and size of fish that anglers can keep.

Both types of fishing are enjoyable and rewarding. Still, anglers must know their impact on the ecosystem and follow responsible fishing practices.

Benefits of Catch-and-Release Fishing

Catch-and-release fishing is recommended because of the following benefits:

- **Conservation**

Catch-and-release fishing helps conserve fish populations by minimizing the number of fish removed from their natural habitat. This fishing method helps maintain the ecosystem's ecological balance and ensures the fish species' survival for future generations.

- **Sustainable Fishing**

By practicing catch-and-release, you are helping to ensure that the fish populations remain healthy and sustainable. This is important for maintaining the integrity of the environment and the health of the fish.

- **Improved Fish Sizes**

Catch-and-release fishing can improve the size and quality of the fish population. By releasing smaller fish, anglers can allow them to grow and mature, leading to larger, healthier fish in the future.

- **Fun and Challenging**

Catch-and-release fishing is fun and challenging for anglers of all experience levels. It allows you to test your skills and enjoy the thrill of the catch without the pressure of keeping the fish.

- **Low Impact**

Catch-and-release fishing has a low environmental impact, as it involves minimal damage to the fish or their habitat. This benefit also helps to maintain the ecosystem's ecological balance and ensures the fish species' survival for future generations.

- **Cultural and Recreational Value**

Fishing is a popular cultural and recreational activity, and catch-and-release fishing allows you to enjoy the experience without negatively impacting the environment or fish populations.

Overall, catch-and-release fishing is a great way to enjoy the thrill of the catch while being mindful of the impact that fishing can have on the environment. By practicing responsible fishing practices, you can help to conserve fish populations and ensure the sustainability of the sport for generations to come.

Drawbacks of Catch-and-Release Fishing

Here are some potential drawbacks of catch-and-release fishing that you may want to consider:

- **Increased Mortality Rate**

Despite best efforts, catch-and-release fishing can result in a mortality rate for the released fish. Handling and hooking injuries, especially in deeply hooked fish, can cause long-term harm, leading to mortality even after releasing the fish back into the water.

- **Stress on Fish**

Catch-and-release fishing can cause significant stress on the fish, making it harder for them to survive after being released. Stress can affect a fish's immune system, making it more vulnerable to disease or predators.

- **Displacement**

Catch-and-release fishing can result in the displacement of fish from their natural habitat, as they may be caught and released in areas that are not optimal for their survival. As a result, this can lead to reduced survival rates and negatively impact the ecosystem.

- **Repeated Capture**

Fish repeatedly caught and released may experience more stress and injury, negatively impacting their health and well-being.

- **Impact on Other Species**

Catch-and-release fishing can have an impact on other species that live in the same environment. For example, predators may be attracted to areas where fish are caught and released, disrupting the ecosystem's natural balance.

It is essential to recognize that catch-and-release fishing has drawbacks, but you can minimize them by practicing responsible fishing. So, ensure proper techniques and equipment are used to help reduce stress and injury on fish and increase their chances of survival after release.

Remember to follow the procedures and precautions we discussed earlier of releasing fish to ensure that you are safeguarding the fish and the ecosystem at large.

Best Practices for Catch and Keep Fishing

Even though catch and release may have many advantages, you may sometimes need to keep the fish for food or other purposes, so you will not return them to the water.

In such a case, here are the best practices you should adhere to:

✓ **Know Your Limits**

Before fishing, familiarize yourself with the fishing regulations and limits for your fishing area. Be sure to adhere to these limits to prevent overfishing and preserve the fish population.

✓ **Choose the Right Gear**

Select fishing gear appropriate for the size and type of fish you plan to catch. Doing this will help minimize injury to the fish, make it easier to handle them, and safely release any unwanted catches.

✓ **Kill the Fish Humanely**

If you plan to keep the fish, kill it as quickly and humanely as possible.

How?

You can do this *using a sharp knife to sever the spinal cord.* Doing so will ensure that the fish does not suffer unnecessarily.

✓ Dispose of Waste Properly

After you have cleaned the fish, dispose of any waste properly to prevent pollution. You can compost fish scraps or dispose of them in a garbage can.

Note: Never dump fish waste in waterways, as it can attract predators and harm the ecosystem.

✓ Respect the Habitat

When fishing, respect the habitat of the fish and avoid disturbing the surrounding environment.

For example, do not damage or remove vegetation, rocks, or other natural features. Instead, stay on designated paths and avoid trampling vegetation or disturbing wildlife.

✓ Use Environmentally-friendly Cleaning Products

If you plan to clean the fish, use environmentally-friendly cleaning products.

Avoid harsh chemicals or bleach, harming aquatic life and polluting the water. Instead, use *natural, biodegradable cleaning agents* such as vinegar or lemon juice.

By following these best practices, you can enjoy fishing while safeguarding the fish population and the environment.

The Impact of Catch-and-Keep on the Ecosystem

Catch-and-keep fishing can have significant impacts on the ecosystem.

Which ones?

When too many fish are caught and removed from a particular body of water, it can disrupt the balance of the ecosystem and lead to *a decline in fish populations*. This decline can have ripple effects throughout the food chain, affecting other aquatic species that rely on fish for food. Furthermore, overfishing can also *impact the health of the water itself*, as fish play an essential role in maintaining the balance of nutrients and oxygen levels in aquatic environments.

In addition to the impact on fish populations, catch-and-keep fishing can contribute to *environmental pollution*. Improper disposal of fish waste can accumulate organic matter in the water, contributing to the growth of harmful algae and other aquatic plants. Additionally, using certain types of fishing gear and equipment can cause physical damage to the habitat and other wildlife in the area.

Therefore, you must practice the responsible fishing techniques we discussed earlier, respect the natural environment, and follow local regulations to help preserve the ecosystem's delicate balance.

Let's move on to the next section and learn how to clean, transport, preserve and cook fish.

SECTION FIVE: CLEANING, TRANSPORTING, PRESERVING, AND COOKING FISH

After deciding to keep your fish, you must clean it before transporting it to your home, factory, or market. After that, the fish will either be preserved to be cooked later or cooked on the spot, in which you will not need to maintain it.

This section will enlighten you about everything you need to do to ensure your catch benefits you as you like.

Let's start with the cleaning of the fish.

Chapter 22: Cleaning, Transporting, and Preserving Fish

1. How to Clean and Prepare Fish for Transport

Here's a step-by-step process on how to clean and prepare fish for transport after fishing:

- **Gather Your Materials**

To clean a fish properly, you will need a few essential tools.

Here are the most common ones and how to use them:

✓ *Fish Scaler*

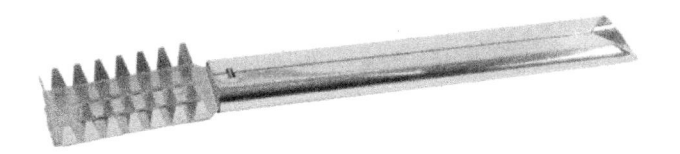

This tool is designed to remove scales from the fish's skin.

You'll use it to scrape the scales from the fish's body, working from tail to head. Doing this will leave the skin smooth and ready for further cleaning.

✓ **Fish Knife**

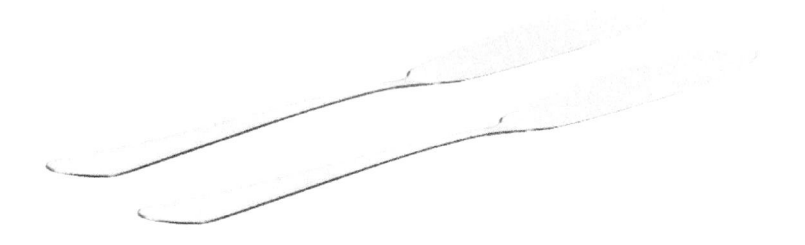

A fish knife has a long, thin, sharp, and flexible blade. The flexible blade is essential for getting into tight spaces and making precise cuts.

You'll use it to remove the fish's head, tail, and fins. You'll also use it to gut the fish and remove any remaining organs, such as the gills and intestines.

✓ ***Cutting Board***

A cutting board is an essential tool for any fish-cleaning task.

Why?

It provides a stable and flat surface to work on and helps prevent the fish from slipping while you're cleaning it.

Choose a board that is large enough to accommodate the size of the fish you'll be cleaning.

✓ **_Tweezers or Pliers_**

These tools remove any remaining bones from the fish after cleaning it.

And how do you do that?

Grip the bone with tweezers or pliers and pull it out of the flesh. This step is likely time-consuming, but removing all the bones is essential, especially if you plan on cooking the fish whole.

✓ **_Bowl of Water_**

Finally, you'll need a water bowl to rinse the fish after cleaning it. The water in the bowl will remove any remaining scales or debris from the skin and flesh.

Be sure to change the water often, especially if cleaning multiple fish.

- **Rinse and Scale the Fish**

Rinse the fish with cool water to remove any debris or blood.

How?

✓ Hold the fish firmly by its tail. Use a fish scaler to scrape the scales from the skin. Work from tail to head, using firm and even pressure. Cover the entire fish surface, including the head, fins, and belly.

✓ After that, rinse the fish under **cold running water** to remove any loose scales.

✓ Use your hands to rub the fish gently and ensure that all the scales have been removed.

- ✓ If there are any remaining scales, use the scaler to remove them.

It's important to note that scaling a fish is messy, so it's a good idea to ***do it outside or in an easy-to-clean area***. You may also want ***gloves*** to protect your hands from the fish's scales.

- **Gut the Fish**

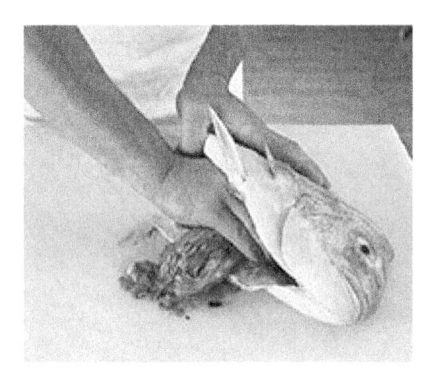

Here is how to gut your catch:

- ✓ Make a small incision along the fish's belly using a knife, from the anus to its gills.

- ✓ Remove the guts and internal organs using a spoon or your fingers.

- ✓ Rinse the inside of the fish with cool water.

- **Remove the Head and Fins**

Use the knife to remove the head of the fish, as well as the fins.

Note: Be careful when handling the fins, as they are sharp.

- **Rinse and Dry the Fish**

Again, rinse the fish with cool water and pat dry with a paper towel or cloth.

- **Fillet the Fish if You Need to**

Filleting a fish involves ***removing the flesh from the bones*** precisely and methodically.

Here is a basic outline of how to fillet your fish:

- ✓ Use a sharp fillet knife to incision behind the fish's gills and backbone.

- ✓ Use the knife to cut along its ribs and remove the fillet from the fish's body. Be sure to cut close to the bones to avoid wasting any of the fish's flesh.

- ✓ Flip the fish over and repeat the process on the other side to remove the second fillet.

- ✓ Once both fillets have been removed, use tweezers or pliers to remove any remaining bones from the flesh.

It's important to note that filleting a fish can take some practice to master. However, by following these basic steps and using a sharp fillet knife, you can quickly and easily remove the flesh from the bones and prepare your fish for cooking or freezing.

- **Place the Fish on some Ice**

Once the fish is cleaned and dried, please keep it in a container with ice.

Why?

The ice will help preserve the freshness of the fish and prevent bacteria from growing.

- **Store the Fish in a cooler or Insulated Bag**

Finally, place the container with the fish on ice in a cooler or insulated bag. Keep the cooler or bag out of direct sunlight and avoid opening it frequently to maintain the fish's temperature and freshness.

2. Importance of Keeping Fish Fresh and Clean

Maintaining the freshness and cleanliness of fish during transport, processing, and storage is crucial for many reasons, including the following:

- **Food Safety**

Proper fish handling is critical to prevent the growth of harmful bacteria and other pathogens that can cause foodborne illnesses. Fish that is not handled correctly can quickly spoil and become unsafe for consumption.

- **Quality**

Keeping fish fresh and clean is vital for maintaining its quality and flavor. Not appropriately handled fish can develop an off taste or odor, making it unpalatable.

- **Sustainability**

Proper handling of fish is also crucial from an environmental perspective. Discarding fish due to spoilage or poor quality results in unnecessary waste and can contribute to overfishing and other environmental issues.

- **Economic Impact**

Proper handling of fish is vital for fishermen and the fishing industry as a whole. Not correctly handling fish can result in lost income and revenue for fishermen and fish markets.

3. How to Preserve and Store Fish for Future Use

Here are the different methods of preserving fish for future use:

- **Freezing**

Freezing is one of the most common and effective methods of preserving fish. It involves ***storing the fish below 0°C***, which inhibits the growth of bacteria and other microorganisms that cause spoilage.

To freeze fish:

✓ First, clean and fillet it.

✓ Wrap it in plastic wrap or freezer paper.

✓ Then, put it in an airtight container.

✓ Label the container with the date and type of fish to ensure freshness and easy identification later.

✓ When ready to use, thaw the fish in the refrigerator overnight.

- **Canning**

Canning is another popular method of preserving fish, especially for those who don't have access to freezing or refrigeration. Canned fish can ***last for years*** without spoiling, making it a convenient and practical option for long-term storage.

To can fish:

✓ First, clean and fillet it, then pack it into sterilized jars.

✓ Add a brine solution made from vinegar, salt, and water.

✓ Seal the jars with lids and process them in a pressure canner according to the manufacturer's instructions.

- **Smoking**

Smoking is a traditional method of preserving fish that extends its shelf life and adds flavor.

The process involves ***exposing the fish to smoke from burning wood*** or other materials, which dries and dehydrates the flesh. Smoked fish could be stored in a cool, dry place for several weeks or longer, depending on the type of fish and the smoking method used.

- **Drying**

Drying is another ancient method of preserving fish that involves removing moisture from the flesh through **exposure to sun, wind, or heat**. Dried fish could be stored for months or even years, making it a popular option for those who live in coastal areas with limited access to refrigeration.

To dry fish:

✓ First, clean and fillet it.

✓ Lay it out on a drying rack in a sunny, breezy spot.

✓ Turn the fish over every few hours until it's dry and brittle.

- **Pickling**

Pickling is a method of preserving fish in **a mixture of vinegar, salt, and spices**, creating a tangy, flavorful product you can store for several months.

To pickle fish:

✓ First, clean and fillet it.

✓ Cut it into bite-sized pieces and pack it into sterilized jars.

✓ Pour the pickling solution over the fish, seal the jars with lids, and store them in a cool, dark place for at least a week before consuming them.

Overall, these methods of preserving and storing fish are great for ensuring that you have access to fresh fish all year round, even when it's out of season or not readily available in your area. By following these simple techniques, you can extend the life of your fish and enjoy it at your convenience.

Let's move to the next chapter and explore how you can cook fish.

Chapter 23: Cooking Fish

Let's say you've managed to reel in a tasty catch, and now you're wondering what to do with it.

Well, fear not because this chapter is all about cooking fish. You'll discover countless ways to prepare and cook fish, each with unique flavor and texture. Whether you're a fan of crispy, grilled fillets or hearty fish stews, this chapter will equip you with the knowledge and skills to turn your fresh catch into a delicious and satisfying meal.

So, grab your apron and prepare to learn exciting new cooking techniques that will make every fishing trip even more rewarding!

How to Season and Marinate Fish

Before we even get into cooking fish, let's learn how to marinate and season fish.

Here is a step-by-step procedure you can use to marinate any fish:

- **Step 1: Choose Your Seasoning and Marinade Ingredients**

Start by selecting the seasonings and marinade ingredients that you want to use.

Popular options include lemon, garlic, ginger, soy sauce, olive oil, salt, and pepper. You can also ***use herbs and spices*** like basil, thyme, rosemary, paprika, and cumin to add flavor.

- **Step 2: Prepare the fish**

Clean and dry the fish before seasoning and marinating. Remove any scales, bones, and other unwanted parts, then pat the fish dry with paper towels.

Step 3: Season the Fish

Generously season the fish with salt and pepper on both sides. Add your choice of herbs and spices to the fish, depending on the flavor you want to achieve.

Step 4: Marinate the Fish

Place the seasoned fish in a shallow dish and pour the marinade. Cover the dish with plastic wrap and let it sit in the refrigerator for at least 30 minutes or up to 2 hours. The longer you marinate the fish, the more flavorful it will be.

After seasoning and marinating, it is now time to cook your fish.

The Three Main Methods of Cooking Fish

You can cook fish either through grilling, baking, or frying. We will explore each method and list the types of fish you can cook using each technique.

Let's dive right in!

1) Grilling Fish

Grilling fish is one of the most popular and simple methods of cooking fish. It is a quick and easy way to cook your catch while preserving its natural flavors and moisture.

Here is a step-by-step guide on how to grill fish like a pro:

- ✓ *Step 1: Preheat Your Grill*

Before you start grilling, preheat your grill to medium-high heat. This step will ensure your fish cooks evenly and doesn't stick to the grill grates.

✓ Step 2: Prepare the Fish

Clean and rinse your fish thoroughly, removing any scales or bones. Pat dry with paper towels, then brush both sides with olive oil to prevent sticking. Lastly, add flavor—season with pepper, salt, and any other desired spices or herbs.

✓ Step 3: Place the Fish on the Grill

Carefully place the fish on the preheated grill, skin side down if it has skin. Close the lid and cook for around 4 minutes on each side, depending on the fish's thickness.

Note: Avoid flipping the fish too often to prevent it from falling apart.

✓ Step 4: Check for Doneness

Check the doneness of your fish by gently pressing it with a fork. The flesh should be **opaque and flake easily**. If it still appears translucent or doesn't flake, let it cook for a few more minutes.

✓ Step 5: Serve and Enjoy

Once your fish is cooked to perfection, carefully remove it from the grill and place it on a plate. Serve with a side of vegetables or rice, and enjoy!

Now that you know how to grill fish, you might wonder which fish species are best suited for this cooking method.

Here are some common types of fish that are great for grilling:

- ✓ Salmon
- ✓ Tuna
- ✓ Swordfish
- ✓ Mahi-mahi
- ✓ Sea bass
- ✓ Trout
- ✓ Snapper
- ✓ Cod

Remember, the key to grilling fish is to **keep it simple and avoid overcooking**. With some practice and patience, you'll be grilling up mouth-watering fish dishes in no time!

2) Baking Fish

Baking fish is a healthy and easy cooking method that allows you to cook your catch with minimal effort.

Here's a step-by-step guide on how to bake fish:

✓ ***Step 1: Preheat the Oven***

Preheat your oven to 375°F (190°C) and adjust the rack to the center position. This step will ensure that your fish cooks evenly.

✓ ***Step 2: Prepare the Fish***

Clean and rinse your fish thoroughly, removing any scales or bones. Pat dry with paper towels, brush both sides with olive oil or melted butter to add flavor and moisture, then season with salt, pepper, and other herbs or spices of your liking.

✓ ***Step 3: Choose Your Baking Dish***

Select a baking dish that is large enough to hold your fish comfortably. You can use a glass or ceramic baking dish or a sheet pan lined with parchment paper.

✓ ***Step 4: Arrange the Fish in the Baking Dish***

Place the fish in the baking dish, skin side down if it has skin. If baking a whole fish, stuff the cavity with herbs, lemon slices, or other aromatic ingredients for added flavor.

✓ **Step 5: Bake the Fish**

Bake the fish in the preheated oven for 12-15 minutes, depending on the thickness of the fish. The flesh should be opaque and flake easily.

Note: Avoid overcooking the fish, which can become dry and tough.

✓ **Step 6: Serve and Enjoy**

Once your fish is baked to perfection, carefully remove it from the oven and place it on a plate. Serve with steamed vegetables or a salad for a healthy and delicious meal!

Now that you know how to bake fish, you might wonder which fish species are best suited for this cooking method.

Here are some common types of fish that are great for baking:

- ✓ Salmon
- ✓ Halibut
- ✓ Tilapia
- ✓ Cod
- ✓ Trout

- ✓ Snapper
- ✓ Sole
- ✓ Catfish

Baking fish is a versatile and easy cooking method that allows you to experiment with different flavors and textures. With practice and creativity, you can turn your fresh catch into a delicious and healthy meal every time!

Baking Fish without the Conventional Oven

Baking fish without a conventional oven is likely challenging, but it is possible with the right tools and techniques.

Here are two ways to bake fish without the conventional oven:

✓ ***Dutch Oven Baking***

If you have a Dutch oven, you can use it for baking fish on a stovetop or over an open fire.

To do this:

- Preheat the Dutch oven over medium heat, and once hot, add the fish and cover with the lid.

- Cook the fish for 10-15 minutes, checking it occasionally to ensure it is not burning.

- Add vegetables, herbs, or other ingredients to the Dutch oven to add flavor.

✓ *Foil Packets*

Another way to bake fish without the conventional oven is to use foil packets.

To do this:

- Place the fish in the center of a large piece of foil.

- Add vegetables, herbs, and spices, as desired, and fold the foil to make a sealed packet.

- Place the packet on a hot grill or a bed of hot coals and cook for 10-15 minutes, checking it occasionally to ensure it is not burning.

While these methods are not quite the same as baking fish in an oven, they can produce delicious results with patience and attention. Be sure to check the fish for doneness by checking that the flesh is opaque and flakey and has reached an internal temperature of 145°F (63°C).

3) Frying Fish

Frying fish is a popular cooking method that produces a crispy and delicious outer layer while keeping the fish moist and tender.

Here's a step-by-step guide to frying fish:

- ✓ **Step 1: Prepare the Fish**

Clean and rinse the fish and pat it dry with a paper towel. Cut the fish into fillets or steaks, and season them with salt and pepper or your favorite seasoning blend.

- ✓ **Step 2: Prepare the Coating**

To get a crispy coating on the fish, you can use breadcrumbs, cornmeal, flour, or a combination of these ingredients. Add herbs, spices, or grated cheese to the coating to add extra flavor.

- ✓ **Step 3: Coat the Fish**

Dip the fish fillets or steaks into a beaten egg mixture, then coat them in the breadcrumb mixture, pressing the coating firmly onto the fish to ensure it sticks.

✓ Step 4: Fry the Fish

Heat a frying pan with about half an inch of oil over medium-high heat. Once the oil is hot, add the fish fillets or steaks to the pan, making sure not to overcrowd the pan. Fry the fish for 2-3 minutes per side until the coating is golden brown and crispy.

✓ Step 5: Drain the Fish

Use a slotted spatula to remove the fish from the pan and place them on a paper towel-lined plate to drain off excess oil.

✓ Step 6: Serve and Enjoy

Serve the fried fish hot with your favorite sides and dipping sauce.

Some of the fish species that you can cook via frying include:

- ✓ Tilapia
- ✓ Catfish
- ✓ Cod
- ✓ Haddock
- ✓ Trout
- ✓ Bass

Remember that the cooking time may vary depending on the fish fillet's or steak's thickness, so adjust the cooking time accordingly. Enjoy your crispy and delicious fried fish!

Top Fish Recipes You Should Try

Now that you know how to cook fish in different ways, here are some excellent fish recipes you should try:

1. Fish Tacos with Delicious Fish Taco Sauce

Serves: 24

Prep Time: Around 30 minutes

Cook Time: Around 25 minutes

Total Time: Around 55 minutes

Nutritional information per serving: Calories- 172 kcal, Fat- 9g, Protein- 8g, Carbs- 15g

Ingredients for the Fish Taco:

1 teaspoon salt

1/2 teaspoon cumin- grounded

1 tablespoon Olive oil

1 tablespoon unsalted butter

1 1/2 lb tilapia

24 small corn tortillas- white

1/2 teaspoon cayenne pepper

1/4 teaspoon black pepper

Toppings for the Fish Taco:

1 lime cut into 8 wedges to serve

2 medium sliced avocados

1/2 bunch of Cilantro whose longer stems have been removed

1/2 diced red onion

1/2 small cabbage-purple cabbage

2 diced Roma tomatoes (optional)

1 cup grated Cotija cheese-4 oz

Ingredients for the Fish Taco Sauce:

1 teaspoon garlic powder

2 tablespoons lime juice

1 teaspoon Sriracha sauce

1/2 cup sour cream

1/3 cup Mayo

Directions:

- ✓ Preheat the oven to 375 degrees F (190 degrees C). Line your baking sheet using a silicone line or parchment paper.

- ✓ Combine the ground cumin, cayenne pepper, salt, and black pepper in a small dish, and sprinkle the mixture on all sides of your fish.

- ✓ Lightly pour the tablespoon of olive oil on the fish and apply butter on each side. Bake in the preheated oven for around 25 minutes, and to brown its edges, broil them for about 5 minutes in the end if need be.

- ✓ Whisk together the sour cream, mayo, lime juice, garlic powder, and Sriracha sauce in a bowl until they blend well.

- ✓ Brown the corn tortillas with high or medium heat on a griddle or dry skillet.

- ✓ To assemble the tacos, start with fish pieces, then add the other ingredients. Lastly, sprinkle a generous amount of the cotija cheese, then your delicious taco sauce!

- ✓ Serve while hot with a lime wedge on the side to use its juice on tacos if desired.

2. Fish Curry

Serves: 4

Prep Time: 5 minutes

Cook Time: 10 minutes

Total Time: 15 minutes

Nutritional Information: Calories- 191 kcal, Fat- 5g, Protein- 30g, Carbs- 9g

Ingredients:

1 chopped garlic clove

1 large chopped onion

1 tablespoon vegetable oil

1-2 tablespoons Madras or Patak's curry paste

200ml vegetable broth

400g can of diced tomatoes

Rice or naan bread

Enough skinned fish fillets, diced into large chunks

Directions:

- ✓ Heat the oil in a pan, then fry the chopped garlic and onion for approximately 5 minutes or until soft.

- ✓ Add the Madras curry paste to the pan and continue to fry as you stir for 1-2 minutes. Then, pour in the diced tomatoes and vegetable stock.

- ✓ Simmer the mixture and add the chunks of fish. Cook under low heat for about 5 minutes until it flakes easily.

- ✓ Serve while hot with naan bread or rice.

3. Fish and Chips

Here's a recipe for making fish and chips:

Serves: 1

Prep time: 20 minutes

Cook time: 35 minutes

Total time: 55 minutes

Nutritional information: Calories-701 kcal, Fat-20g, Protein-54g, Carbs-72g

Ingredients needed to cook the Fish:

1 pinch of ground black pepper

1 teaspoon baking powder

1/3 cup cold dark beer

1/3 cup cold sparkling water

4 (7-ounce) thick fish fillets (white fish)

7 tablespoons (55 grams) of all-purpose flour, placed separately

7 tablespoons (55 grams) cornstarch

Sea salt, to taste

Ingredients needed to cook the Chips:

A liter of lard or vegetable oil

2 pounds potatoes, peeled

Directions:

- ✓ Keep aside 2 tablespoons of the all-purpose flour. Mix the remaining 5 tablespoons of flour with the baking powder, salt, cornstarch, and pepper in a large bowl.

- ✓ Add the sparkling water and beer to the mixture and whisk continuously with a fork until a thick, smooth mixture forms. Keep the mixture in the fridge for 30 minutes to 1 hour.

- ✓ Chop the potatoes into slices about 1/2-inch-thick and then slice them further into chips of about 1/2-inch-width. Put them into a colander, then rinse them with cold running water.

- ✓ Put the washed chips in a pan with cold water. Let them have a gentle boil, then simmer for about 4 minutes. Use a colander to drain them carefully, then use paper towels to dry them. Cover them with dry paper towels, then put them in the fridge until needed.

- ✓ Place your fish fillets on a clean paper towel, pat dry, and season with sea salt.

- ✓ Pour the oil into a large deep saucepan or deep-fat fryer and heat it to 350 F. Take handfuls of the chips and cook them in the oil for 2 minutes. However, do not let them brown. Once slightly cooked, scoop your chips from the fryer or pan and drain. Set them aside.

- ✓ Put the flour you set aside (the 2 tablespoons) into a bowl. Place your fish fillet in the bowl of flour and gently pat off any excess. Dip the fillets into the mixture you put in the fridge, ensuring to coat all the fillets entirely.

- ✓ Lower the fillets into the dryer or oil with the oil temperature still at 350 F. Fry until the batter is golden and crisp, which should take around 8 minutes. Remember to turn them over occasionally.

- ✓ Once ready, remove your fillets from the fryer or pan and use paper towels to drain them. Sprinkle some salt n the fillets, then cover them with greaseproof paper.

- ✓ Increase the heat to 400 F, add the chips to the oil, then let them cook until crisp and golden, which should be about 5 minutes. Once ready, drain the chips from the fryer or pan, then use salt to season.

- ✓ Serve your chips and fish while hot, accompanied by a salad of your liking.

Now that you know how to cook fish differently, let's move to the last section of this book, where we will learn about boats and how to be a responsible boater when fishing.

SECTION SIX: BOATS AND MOTORS

Regardless of your skill level in fishing, one of the essential tools at your disposal is a reliable boat with an efficient motor. **Boats** provide access to areas of water that are otherwise inaccessible from the shore, and **motors** help you move around quickly and efficiently.

However,

Choosing the right one is likely overwhelming, with many boats and motors available. In this chapter, we'll guide you through everything you need to know about boats and motors for fishing, from choosing the right boat and motor to maintaining them for optimal performance.

The Importance of Having High-Quality Boats and Motors

The right boat and motor are crucial for a successful and enjoyable fishing experience.

Here are some reasons why you should invest in a high-quality boat and motor:

- **Access to Remote Fishing Spots**

A boat allows you to access remote fishing spots that are difficult or impossible to reach on foot.

Hence,

With the right boat, you can explore new fishing grounds and increase your chances of catching more fish.

- **Increased Mobility**

A motorized boat provides increased mobility and allows you to move quickly and efficiently around the water. This mobility is significant, especially when fishing in large bodies of water where fish may be scattered over a wide area.

- **Improved Safety**

A high-quality boat and motor can provide improved safety while fishing. A sturdy boat with a reliable motor can help you navigate rough waters and withstand unexpected weather conditions.

- **Comfort and Convenience**

A comfortable and well-equipped boat can make your fishing trip more enjoyable and convenient. Having ample storage space, comfortable seating, and other amenities can help you focus on fishing rather than worrying about equipment or discomfort.

- **Cost-Effective**

Investing in a high-quality boat and the best motor is cost-effective in the long run. A reliable boat and motor will require less maintenance and repairs, saving you money.

That said,

Let's explore the different boat types to help you make the best choice.

Chapter 24: Types of Boats

When you are a beginner in fishing, it is likely overwhelming to choose between different types of boats for fishing.

However, you do not need to worry; in this chapter, we will explore the different types of boats along with the pros and cons of each.

1. Kayaks

A kayak is a small, narrow boat propelled using a double-bladed paddle. It is a popular choice for fishing due to its *versatility and ability to access remote fishing spots*.

Kayaks are usually made of lightweight materials such as plastic, fiberglass, or Kevlar, which makes them easy to transport and store.

- **Pros of Kayak Fishing**

Here are the benefits of using a Kayak boat:

- ✓ **Affordability**: Kayaks are generally less expensive than other fishing boats, making them an excellent option for beginners on a budget.
- ✓ **Versatility**: Kayaks are used in freshwater and saltwater environments, and their small size `and maneuverability

make them ideal for fishing in tight spots, such as around rocks, logs, or other obstructions.

- ✓ **Accessibility**: Kayaks can easily access remote or difficult-to-reach fishing locations that are not accessible by larger boats.

- ✓ **Stealth:** Because kayaks are quiet and sit low in the water, they allow you to sneak up on fish and catch them without disturbing the surrounding water.

- ✓ **Exercise**: Kayak fishing provides a low-impact exercise that improves cardiovascular health, strengthens core muscles, and helps reduce stress.

- **Cons of Kayak Fishing**

The disadvantages of using a Kayak boat include the following:

- ✓ **Limited space:** Kayaks are small, so there is limited space for gear, which may make it difficult to carry all the equipment you need for a long day of fishing.

- ✓ **Exposure:** Kayaks offer little protection from the elements, exposing you to the sun, wind, and rain.

- ✓ **Safety concerns:** Kayaks can capsize, and you must know how to swim and use a personal flotation device (PFD) to ensure your safety. Additionally, you must be aware of tides, currents, and other weather conditions that may impact your fishing safety.

- ✓ **Limited mobility:** Kayaks require manual paddling, which is likely tiring and limits mobility. You may also have difficulty navigating in strong currents or winds.

- ✓ **Limited stability**: Due to their narrow design, kayaks have less strength than larger boats, making it challenging to stand up or move around while fishing.

2. Canoes

A canoe is a lightweight boat typically open on the top and propelled using a single-bladed paddle. It is a popular choice for fishing due to *its versatility and ability to navigate through shallow waters*. Canoes are often made of wood, aluminum, or lightweight composite materials.

- **Pros of Using Canoes for Fishing**

- ✓ **Affordability:** Compared to other fishing boats, canoes are generally less expensive, making them an excellent option for beginners on a budget.

- ✓ **Versatility:** Canoes are used in freshwater and saltwater environments and are ideal for navigating shallow water and small streams.

- ✓ **Accessibility:** Canoes can easily access remote or difficult-to-reach fishing locations that are not accessible by larger boats.

- ✓ **Stealth:** Canoes are quiet and sit low in the water, allowing you to approach fish without disturbing them.

- ✓ **Exercise:** Canoe fishing provides a low-impact exercise that improves cardiovascular health, strengthens core muscles, and helps reduce stress.

- **Cons of Using Canoes when Fishing**

- ✓ **Limited space:** Canoes are small, so there is limited space for gear, which may make it difficult to carry all the equipment you need for a long day of fishing.

- ✓ **Exposure:** Canoes offer little protection from the elements, exposing you to the sun, wind, and rain.

- ✓ **Safety concerns:** Canoes can capsize, and you must know how to swim and use a personal flotation device (PFD) to ensure your safety. Additionally, you must be aware of tides, currents, and other weather conditions that may impact your fishing safety.

- ✓ **Limited mobility:** Canoes require manual paddling, which is likely tiring and limits your mobility. You may also have difficulty navigating in strong currents or winds.

✓ **Limited stability:** Due to their narrow design, canoes have less strength than larger boats, making it challenging to stand up or move around while fishing.

3. Jon Boats

A Jon boat is a small, flat-bottomed boat ideal for fishing in calm waters. It is a popular choice for fishing due to *its stability and affordability*.

Jon boats are typically made of aluminum, fiberglass, or wood and come in various sizes.

- **Pros of Jon Boat Fishing**

The pros of fishing with a Jon boat are:

✓ **Affordability:** Jon boats are generally less expensive than larger fishing boats, making them an excellent option for beginners on a budget.

✓ **Stability:** Jon boats have a flat bottom, which makes them very stable and unlikely to tip over.

✓ **Maneuverability:** Jon boats are easy to maneuver in shallow waters, making them ideal for fishing in small streams or ponds.

- ✓ **Customizability:** You can customize your Jon boat with accessories such as trolling motors, fish finders, and Live Wells to make your fishing experience more efficient and enjoyable.

- ✓ **Easy to maintain:** Jon boats are typically low-maintenance and require little upkeep, saving you time and money in the long run.

- **Cons of Jon Boat Fishing:**

They include the following:

- ✓ **Limited space:** Jon boats are relatively small, so there is limited space for gear and passengers.

- ✓ **Exposure:** Jon boats offer little protection from the elements, exposing you to the sun, wind, and rain.

- ✓ **Limited range:** Jon boats are best suited for calm waters and are not ideal for use in rough seas or large bodies of water.

- ✓ **Limited speed:** Jon boats are not designed for speed, which may limit your ability to cover larger water areas.

- ✓ **Little comfort:** Jon boats are not known for their comfort, and you may experience some discomfort during long fishing trips.

4. Bass Boats

A bass boat is a specialized fishing boat designed primarily for bass fishing. It is typically a small, ***high-powered*** boat with a flat deck and ***a low profile*** that allows it to move quickly through the water.

Bass boats often have features like fish finders, Live Wells, and trolling motors.

- **Pros of Bass Boat Fishing**

They include:

- ✓ **Speed**: Bass boats are designed for speed and can quickly cover large areas of water, making them ideal for tournament fishing or fishing in larger bodies of water.

- ✓ **Maneuverability**: Bass boats are highly maneuverable, allowing you to navigate through narrow channels and tight spaces.

- ✓ **Comfort**: Bass boats often have comfortable seating and amenities such as shade covers and drink holders, making your fishing experience more enjoyable.

- ✓ **Fishing features**: Bass boats often have fish finders, Live Wells, and other elements that can help you locate and catch fish more efficiently.

- ✓ **Customizability**: you can customize your bass boat with various features and accessories, allowing you to create the perfect fishing setup for your needs.

- **Cons of Bass Boat Fishing**

The cons of fishing with a bass boat are:

- ✓ **Cost**: Bass boats are expensive, making them a significant investment for beginners on a budget.

- ✓ **Limited access**: Bass boats are not well-suited for fishing in shallow waters or small streams, limiting your access to specific fishing locations.

- ✓ **Maintenance**: Bass boats require regular maintenance and upkeep, which is likely time-consuming and costly.

- ✓ **Safety concerns**: Bass boats travel at high speeds, and you must be aware of safety concerns, such as wakes and other boats on the water.

- ✓ **Environmental impact**: Bass boats can negatively impact the environment, particularly in sensitive areas where noise and pollution disrupt local wildlife.

5. Pontoon Boats

A pontoon boat is a type of boat that is designed with a flat platform that sits on top of two or more pontoons (large diameter tubes) that are filled with air. You propel it with a motor and steer it by a steering wheel or tiller.

They are generally used for recreational purposes like fishing, cruising, and water sports.

- **Pros of Using a Pontoon Boat for Fishing**

✓ **Stability:** Pontoon boats are known for their strength on the water. The vast and flat design of the boat makes it less likely to tip over, which is especially important for those new to boating.

✓ **Space:** Pontoon boats are spacious and can accommodate many people. This benefit makes them ideal for group fishing trips, where you can invite your friends and family to join you on the boat.

✓ **Comfort**: Pontoon boats are comfortable and often have comfortable seating, a canopy to provide shade, and a built-in cooler to keep your drinks and snacks cold.

- ✓ **Versatility:** Pontoon boats are used for various water activities, not just fishing. You can use them for cruising, water sports, and camping trips.

- **Cons of Using a Pontoon Boat for Fishing**

- ✓ **Speed**: Pontoon boats are not known for their speed. They are generally slower than other boats, which may be a disadvantage if you plan to cover a large water area.

- ✓ **Maneuverability:** Pontoon boats are not as maneuverable as other boats, such as bass boats or kayaks. This con may make navigating through tight spaces or shallow waters challenging.

- ✓ **Wind:** Due to their flat design, pontoon boats are more susceptible to wind than other boats. This characteristic may make keeping the boat in place when fishing challenging.

- ✓ **Cost:** Pontoon boats are expensive, especially if you want to purchase a new one. Additionally, you will need to consider the cost of maintenance, storage, and fuel.

How to Choose the Right Boat

Choosing the right boat for fishing is crucial for your comfort and success while on the water.

As a beginner angler, here are several factors you need to consider before making a purchase:

- **Budget**

The first factor to consider is your budget. Boats come in a wide range of prices, so it's essential to set a budget and stick to it.

Remember that owning a boat also comes with additional costs, such as maintenance, storage, and fuel.

- **Size**

The size of the boat is another essential factor to consider.

Smaller boats are more affordable and easier to handle, but they may not be suitable for larger bodies of water or if you plan on bringing more people. On the other hand, larger boats offer more space and stability, but they are likely more challenging to navigate.

- **Type of Water Body**

The type of water body you plan to fish in is another crucial factor.

A small boat or kayak may be more suitable if you plan to fish in small rivers or lakes. You may need a larger boat with a more powerful motor for larger bodies of water, such as oceans or large lakes.

- **Type of Fishing**

The type of fishing you plan to do is also essential to consider.

If you plan on trolling or casting, a boat with a trolling motor may be necessary. A smaller boat or kayak may be more suitable for fly fishing.

- **Comfort**

Comfort is crucial when spending long hours on the water. Consider comfortable seating, shade, and storage for your gear and refreshments when choosing your boat.

- **Safety**

Safety should always be a top priority when choosing a boat.

Therefore,

Look for boats with safety features such as life jackets, fire extinguishers, and emergency signaling devices.

- **Maneuverability**

The maneuverability of the boat is also essential. Consider how easy it is to handle the boat, how it turns, and how it navigates through shallow waters.

- **Storage**

Consider where you plan on storing the boat when not in use. A smaller or inflatable boat may be more practical with limited space.

- **Type of Boat**

There are many types of boats available for fishing, including pontoons, bass boats, center consoles, and kayaks. Each boat has advantages and disadvantages, so research each type and determine which is best for your needs.

Let's move on to the next chapter and learn about boat safety and maintenance.

Chapter 25: Boat Safety and Maintenance

After choosing the right boat for your fishing adventure, you must stay safe while in the waters.

So,

Let's look at what you should do to guarantee and enhance your safety when in water with a boat.

Tips for Staying Safe when Boat Fishing

Here are a few tips to help improve your safety while fishing on a boat:

- **Wear a Life Jacket**

Ensure you wear a properly fitted life jacket that the Coast Guard to your area approves. Even if you're a strong swimmer, a life jacket can keep you afloat in an emergency.

- **Check the Weather Forecast**

Always check the weather forecast before you head out. If there are high winds, waves, or a chance of storms, consider postponing your trip.

- **Bring Safety Equipment**

Here is a list of safety items you should carry on a boat when going fishing and their purposes:

✓ *Life Jackets*

Life jackets are the essential safety item on board. They are designed to keep you afloat in the water and could be the difference between life and death in an emergency.

✓ *First Aid Kit*

This kit should contain basic medical supplies such as bandages, antiseptics, and pain relievers. It is essential for treating minor injuries and can also be used to stabilize more severe injuries before professional help arrives.

✓ *Flares*

Flares are used to signal for help in an emergency. They are bright and seen from a distance, making them an effective way to get attention.

✓ **Fire Extinguisher**

A fire extinguisher puts out small fires before they become big problems.

✓ **Whistle**

Whistle signals for help or can get someone's attention. It is a simple but effective way to communicate in an emergency.

✓ Anchor and Anchor Line

An anchor is used to keep your boat in place when fishing or in case of an emergency. Make sure that the anchor line is long enough to reach the bottom.

✓ Navigation Lights

Navigation lights are required by law and help other boaters see you at night or in low visibility conditions.

✓ GPS Chart Plotter

A GPS chart plotter can help you navigate and keep track of your position. It is beneficial, especially when fishing in unfamiliar waters.

✓ Radio

A VHF radio is used to communicate with other boats or authorities in an emergency.

- **Tell Someone Your Plans**

Let someone know where you are going and when you plan to return.

This way,

If you don't return as planned, someone can alert authorities.

- **Stay Seated while the Boat is moving**

When the boat moves, stay seated and keep your center of gravity low. Following this tip can help you avoid falls and injuries.

- **Avoid Alcohol**

Never drink alcohol while on the boat.

Here is why:

It can impair your judgment, balance, and coordination, making accidents more likely.

- **Keep a Lookout**

Always watch for other boats, obstacles, and changes in the weather. Use your senses to stay aware of your surroundings.

- **Practice Safe Fishing Techniques**

Keep fishing lines and hooks away from others, and always wear protective clothing, such as gloves and sunglasses.

Another way you can enhance your safety is by ensuring that your boat is properly maintained.

Let's cover that in the section below.

How to Maintain Your Boat

Here are a few tips on how you can ensure proper maintenance of your boat:

1. Wash and Rinse your Boat after Each Use

After fishing, wash and rinse your boat thoroughly with fresh water. This maintenance tip will help remove salt, dirt, and other debris that can damage your boat's exterior.

2. Change Your Boat's Oil and Filters Regularly

Like your car, your boat's engine needs regular oil changes and filter replacements. Check your boat's manual for the recommended maintenance schedule and follow it.

3. Check Your Boat's Battery

The battery is a crucial component of your boat's electrical system. Check the battery regularly for corrosion, leaks, and signs of wear.

Ensure the connections are clean and tight and the battery is fully charged.

4. Inspect Your Boat's Propeller

The propeller is responsible for propelling your boat through the water. Check it regularly for damage, such as nicks, dings, and cracks.

Make sure the propeller is installed correctly and securely attached.

5. Keep Your Boat's Bilge Clean

The bilge is the lowest part of your boat's hull, where water accumulates. Please keep it clean and debris-free, as this can interfere with your boat's performance.

6. Check Your Boat's Fuel System

The fuel system is responsible for delivering fuel to your boat's engine. Check the fuel lines, tanks, and filters regularly for leaks, cracks, and other signs of wear.

Make sure to replace any damaged components as soon as possible.

7. Keep Your Boat Covered when Not in Use

Environmental exposure, such as sun or rain, can damage your boat's exterior and interior.

So,

Cover your boat when not in use to protect it from the sun, wind, rain, and other weather conditions.

By following these tips, you can help ensure that your boat remains in good condition and is safe for fishing. Regular maintenance can also help prevent costly repairs and prolong the life of your boat.

Let's now move on to the next chapter and learn about motors.

Chapter 26: Motors; Everything You Need to Know

If you're new to fishing, you may wonder why boats need motors.

Well, here is the answer,

Motors are used **to power boats** through the water, allowing you to reach fishing spots that would be difficult or impossible to get otherwise. Boats with motors can move faster and farther than those powered solely by oars or paddles.

Motors come in various sizes and types, from small electric trolling motors to powerful outboard motors that can propel a boat at high speeds.

This chapter will explore the different types of motors commonly used on fishing boats and their respective advantages and disadvantages.

And,

By the end, you'll better understand why motors are crucial to fishing boats.

- **Different Types of Motors**

There are several different types to consider when it comes to motors for fishing boats.

Below are the most common types you can use, along with their pros and cons:

1. Electric Motors

Electric boat motors are a type of motor that is **powered by batteries** and used to propel boats through the water. If you're considering using an electric motor for your fishing boat, it's crucial to understand how they work.

And how do they work?

Electric boat motors **convert electrical energy** from the battery *into mechanical energy* that moves the propeller, which propels the boat forward. The motor is connected to the battery and a control system that regulates the motor's speed and direction. When you turn on the motor, the battery sends an electrical current to the motor, spinning the propeller and moving the boat forward.

Below are the pros and cons of electric motors:

Pros:

- ✓ Quiet operation
- ✓ Environmentally friendly and produce no exhaust fumes
- ✓ Low maintenance requirements

- ✓ Ideal for small to medium-sized boats
- ✓ You can use it for trolling or as a backup motor

Cons:

- ✓ Limited speed and range compared to gas motors
- ✓ Require frequent battery recharging
- ✓ It may not be suitable for larger boats or rough waters

2. **Gas Motors**

Gas boat motors, or gasoline-powered motors, are another type commonly used in fishing boats. If you're considering using a gas motor for your boat, it's essential to understand how they work.

So here is how:

Gas boat motors ***use gasoline to power*** an internal combustion engine, which drives a propeller that moves the boat through the water. When you turn on the motor, gasoline is injected into the engine's cylinders, where a spark plug ignites it. This explosion creates pressure that drives a piston, which operates the propeller.

Below are the pros and cons of gas motors:

Pros:

- ✓ More powerful than electric motors
- ✓ It can provide more incredible speed and range
- ✓ Ideal for larger boats
- ✓ Can handle rough waters and adverse weather conditions
- ✓ Easy to refuel

Cons:

- ✓ Noisy operation
- ✓ Produce exhaust fumes and contribute to air and water pollution
- ✓ Require regular maintenance
- ✓ Higher operating costs due to fuel consumption

3. Trolling Motors

Trolling boat motors are a type of motor that is designed explicitly for ***slow-speed fishing***. If you're considering using a trolling motor for your fishing boat, it's essential to understand how they work.

Here is how:

Trolling boat motors use **an electric motor and a propeller** to move the boat through the water slowly and steadily. They are typically mounted on the bow or stern of the boat and are controlled using a foot pedal or remote control. This feature allows you to control the speed and direction of the boat precisely, making it easier to target specific areas for fishing.

Below are the pros and cons of these motors:

Pros:

- ✓ Designed explicitly for slow-speed fishing
- ✓ Precise speed control using a foot pedal or remote control
- ✓ Quiet operation
- ✓ Low maintenance requirements
- ✓ You can use it in conjunction with other motors

Cons:

- ✓ Limited speed and range compared to gas motors
- ✓ It may not be powerful enough for larger boats or strong currents
- ✓ Battery life is likely negligible, requiring frequent recharging

- ✓ It may not be suitable for rough waters or adverse weather conditions

- **How to Choose the Right Type of Motor for Your Boat and Fishing Style**

Choosing the suitable motor for your boat will determine how smooth and successful your fishing trip will be.

Here are vital factors you should consider:

✓ **Boat Size and Weight**

The size and weight of your boat will determine which motor is suitable for your boat.

Electric trolling motors are often the best option for ***smaller boats***, such as kayaks and canoes, due to their low weight and quiet operation. ***Gas-powered motors*** are better for ***larger boats***, as they provide more power and speed.

✓ **Water Conditions**

The type of water you'll be fishing in will also influence your choice of motor.

Electric trolling motors are often sufficient for *calm waters* like lakes and ponds. *Gas motors* are better suited for *rougher waters*, such as coastal areas or open seas, as they provide the necessary power to navigate waves and currents.

✓ **Fishing Style**

Your preferred fishing style will also impact your choice of motor.

Electric trolling motors are the best choice for anglers who prefer to *fish stationarily*, such as when fly-fishing or baitcasting. *Gas motors* are better for anglers who prefer to *cover more water* and fish on the move.

✓ **Fuel Efficiency**

If you plan on fishing for long periods, fuel efficiency is an essential factor to consider.

Electric trolling motors are the *most fuel-efficient* option, as they are powered by batteries that you can recharge. Gas motors are less fuel-efficient but provide more power and speed.

✓ **Environmental Impact**

Finally, it's essential to consider the environmental impact of your choice of motor.

Electric trolling motors are the ***most environmentally friendly*** option, producing no exhaust fumes or pollution. On the other hand, gas motors have exhaust fumes and contribute to air and water pollution.

After choosing the suitable motor, you must ensure it is well-maintained to serve you for as long as possible.

But how do you do that?

Let's find out.

- ## How to Maintain Boat Motors

Maintaining your boat motor is crucial to ensuring it operates efficiently and reliably.

Here are a few tips to help you keep your boat motor in top condition, along with which information is suitable for which types of motors:

✓ **Keep the Motor Clean**

Regularly clean your motor to prevent dirt and debris from accumulating. This maintenance tip is significant, especially for ***gas motors***, which can develop blockages in the fuel lines or carburetor if not adequately maintained.

✓ **Check the Oil Levels**

Regularly check your motor's oil levels to ensure sufficient lubrication. This tip is vital for both ***gas and electric motors.***

✓ **Check the Propeller**

Inspect the propeller for damage or wear, and replace it if necessary. This maintenance tip is essential, especially for ***gas motors***, which can become damaged if the propeller strikes rocks or other objects.

✓ **Change the Spark Plugs**

Replace the spark plugs on your gas motor regularly to ensure it operates efficiently. Doing this will also help prevent starting issues and poor performance.

✓ **Charge the Battery**

If you have ***an electric motor***, make sure to keep the battery charged and in good condition. Doing this will ensure your motor has sufficient power to operate.

✓ **Flush the Motor**

After use, flush your motor with fresh water to remove salt and other contaminants. This tip is vital, especially for ***gas motors*** in saltwater environments, as salt can cause corrosion and further damage.

✓ Follow the Manufacturer's Instructions

Finally, following the manufacturer's instructions for maintaining your specific motor is essential. It will ensure you use the correct lubricants, fuel, and other maintenance procedures.

Let's move on to the next chapter and learn about boat accessories.

Chapter 27: Boat Accessories

As a beginner in fishing, you may have already invested in a boat, motor, and fishing gear. However, to fully enjoy your time on the water, you must consider adding boat accessories to your setup

Boat accessories are additional items that can help improve your overall boating experience, whether by increasing safety, convenience, or functionality.

This chapter will cover the different types of boat accessories available, how to maintain them, and what they are used for so you can make informed decisions about which accessories to add to your fishing arsenal.

Different Fishing Accessories and How to Maintain Them

- **Trolling Plates**

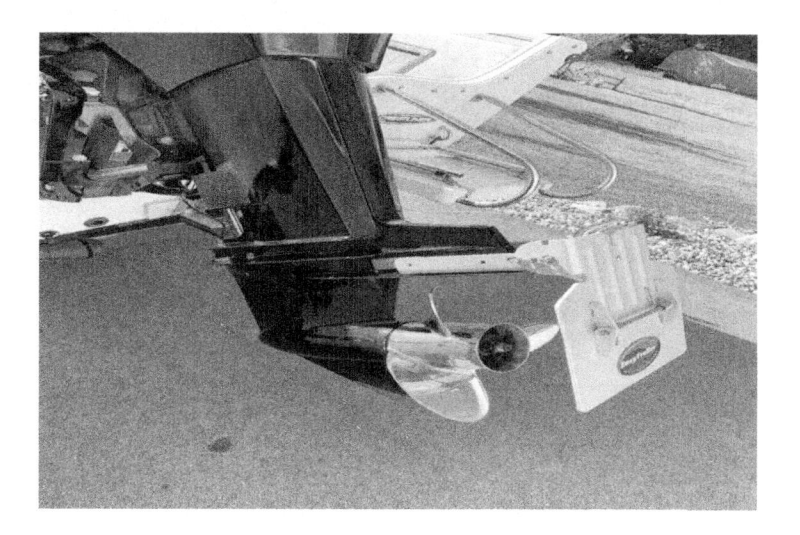

A trolling plate is a device that **attaches to your motor to slow down your boat** when trolling. It can help you maintain a consistent speed and reduce noise and vibration.

To maintain your trolling plate, clean it after each use and inspect it for any damage or wear.

- **Boat Seats**

A comfortable boat seat can help you stay on the water for extended periods without discomfort.

To maintain your boat seat, regularly clean it with mild soap and water and protect it from prolonged exposure to sunlight

- **Fish Finders**

As discussed earlier, a fish finder is an electronic device that uses sonar to detect fish in the water. It can help you locate fish and determine their depth and size.

To maintain your fish finder, regularly clean the screen and correctly calibrate it.

- **Anchors**

An anchor is a device that secures your boat in one place. This accessory is essential when you want to fish at a specific point in the water.

To maintain your anchor, rinse it with fresh water after each use to prevent corrosion.

- **Downrigger**

A downrigger is a device that **helps you to fish at specific depths** by attaching a weight to a line and then lowering it down into the water. It's a valuable accessory for trolling and can help you catch fish deeper in the water column.

To maintain your downrigger, rinse it with fresh water after each use and store it in a dry place.

- **Rod Holders**

Rod holders **hold fishing rods in place** while you fish. They are mounted on the boat and come in different shapes and sizes. They are helpful when you have multiple lines in the water or need a break from holding the rod.

To maintain your rod holders, clean them after each use and check for any signs of wear or damage.

- **Live Well**

A Live Well is *a tank on your boat holding live bait or catch*. It keeps the fish alive and healthy until you're ready to clean or release them.

For maintenance, clean this accessory regularly and add fresh water and oxygen as needed. Keeping the Live Well aerated is also essential to prevent the fish from suffocating.

How to Choose the Right Accessories for Your Boat and Fishing Style

As a beginner in fishing, choosing the right accessories for your boat and fishing style is likely overwhelming.

And so,

Here are some factors to consider when selecting accessories:

- **Boat Size and Type**

The type and size of the boat you have will determine which accessories are appropriate. For example, a larger boat may require a bigger anchor, while a smaller boat may not need a trolling plate.

It's important to choose accessories that are compatible with your boat.

- **Fishing Style**

The type of fishing you plan to do will also impact which accessories you need. For example, a trolling plate and downrigger may be helpful if you plan to do a lot of trolling. If you plan to do more casting, rod holders and a Live Well may be more significant.

Think about the specific needs of your fishing style when selecting accessories.

- **Budget**

Accessories can range in price, so it's essential to consider your budget when selecting them.

You may not need the most expensive accessories for a successful fishing trip, but you don't want to skimp on important safety or functionality features.

- **Durability**

It's important to select accessories that are durable and built to withstand the wear and tear of being on the water. Look for accessories made from high-quality materials that will last for many fishing trips to come.

- **Ease of Use**

Some accessories may be more complex to use than others. Consider your comfort level with technology and the ease of use of different accessories when selecting.

Having learned about boat accessories, let's move on to the last chapter and learn about licensing, regulations, and etiquette you should follow when fishing.

Chapter 28: Etiquette, Licensing, and Regulations for Fishing

Before you grab your fishing rod and head out to the nearest body of water, it's essential to understand the etiquette, licensing, and regulations involved in fishing.

Are you aware of the licensing requirements in your area?

This chapter will provide a comprehensive guide to the do's and don'ts of fishing and the legal and ethical considerations you need to be aware of before you cast your line.

- **Licensing Requirements for Fishing**

As a beginner in fishing, it's essential to understand the licensing requirements in different regions to avoid legal issues while enjoying your favorite pastime.

The licensing requirements vary widely depending on the region and could be as specific as requiring a license for fishing in a particular lake or river.

Let's look at licensing requirements for a few regions:

1. The United States

Here are some examples of the different licensing requirements for fishing in the United States:

✓ *Freshwater Fishing Only*

Some states, such as Colorado, offer licenses for freshwater fishing only. This means you can fish in rivers, lakes, and streams but not in the ocean or other bodies of saltwater.

✓ *Saltwater Fishing*

States such as Florida, surrounded by water on three sides, require a saltwater fishing license and a freshwater license. This allows you to fish in the ocean and other saltwater bodies.

✓ *Combination License*

Other states, like California, offer a combination license allowing you to fish in freshwater and saltwater. A combination license is more expensive than freshwater but provides more opportunities to fish in different locations.

✓ *Different Licenses for Different Species*

Some states, like Texas, require different licenses for different types of fishing. For example, a license to catch freshwater fish is separate from a license to catch saltwater fish, and there may be other licenses required for fishing for certain species, such as trout or salmon.

It's important to note that licensing requirements can vary even within a state, so it's always best to check with the local authorities or fishing organizations for specific information.

Some states also offer exemptions from licensing requirements for certain groups, such as senior citizens or individuals with disabilities. Again, it's always best to check with the local authorities to determine if you qualify for exemptions.

2. Europe

Europe is a diverse continent with varying licensing requirements for fishing.

✓ United Kingdom

In the United Kingdom, for example, you need a rod fishing license to fish for freshwater fish, such as trout, salmon, and coarse fish, in England, Wales, and the Scottish borders.

- ✓ *Ireland*

In Ireland, you'll require a permit or a license to fish for coarse fish in public waters, while in Scotland, you need a permit to fish for migratory fish like salmon or sea trout.

- ✓ *France*

In France, a fishing license is required to fish in freshwater and saltwater, while in *Spain,* a fishing license is only required for certain species, such as trout, salmon, and eels.

Additional permits or permissions may be required to fish in some areas, such as national parks, wildlife reserves, or private lakes.

It is important to note that fishing license requirements can change yearly. So, checking with the relevant authorities is essential to ensure you have the appropriate permits and licenses before fishing in a new area.

You may not need a fishing license in some regions, such as private lakes or specific areas within national parks. However, it is vital to research the rules and regulations before fishing in any place to avoid breaking the law.

- **Other Common Regulations for Fishing**

As an avid fisherman, you must follow several rules and regulations to ensure the sustainability of fish populations and protect the environment.

Here are some standard regulations that apply to most regions:

✓ **Size Limits**

Many regions have specific size limits for certain species of fish. This regulation means that you can only keep fish that are above a particular size, and you need to release any fish that are smaller than that size.

Why?

The purpose of size limits is to allow fish to reach maturity and reproduce, which helps to maintain healthy fish populations.

✓ **Bag Limits**

Bag limits refer to the number of fish you can catch and keep daily. Many regions have bag limits to prevent overfishing and ensure that there are enough fish to sustain the population.

Check the bag limits for the species you plan to target before you head out.

✓ **Catch and Release**

Catch-and-release is when you catch a fish and then release it back into the water rather than keeping it. Catch-and-release is essential for maintaining healthy fish populations, especially for overfished or threatened species.

When practicing catch-and-release, handle the fish carefully and release it quickly to minimize stress and improve its chances of survival.

✓ **No Fishing Zones**

Some regions have designated areas where fishing is prohibited. These areas may be set aside for environmental conservation, scientific research, or recreational activities.

Check for no-fishing zones where you plan to fish, and respect these rules to avoid fines or penalties.

✓ **Use of Artificial Lures Only**

In some areas, live bait or specific lures may be prohibited to protect the local ecosystem. Instead, you may be required to use artificial lures, which are less likely to harm the fish or the environment.

- ✓ **Fishing Permits and Licenses**

Fishing permits and licenses are required in most regions, and they help ensure that fishing is sustainable and properly regulated. Ensure you obtain the necessary permits and licenses before fishing; always carry them with you.

These are just a few of the many regulations that apply to fishing. Depending on the region where you plan to fish, there may be additional rules and regulations that you need to follow. It's always a good idea to research the regulations for your area before you head out and to ensure you understand and follow all of the rules to protect the environment and maintain healthy fish populations.

- **Etiquette on Water and Why It's Important**

When fishing, there are some etiquettes you should uphold to make your experience and that of other people sharing the water with you easy and enjoyable.

Here are some etiquettes you should uphold and why they are essential:

1. Respect other Fishermen

When fishing, it's essential to be considerate of other anglers on the water.

For example, avoid fishing too close to others or casting over their lines. Give them plenty of space, so they can enjoy their fishing experience as much as you want yours.

2. Keep Your Noise Level Down

Loud noises and music is likely disruptive to other fishermen on the water. Keep your noise level down so you don't disturb other anglers' peace.

3. Dispose of Trash Properly

Leaving trash behind is not only bad for the environment but also ruins the beauty of the waterways.

So,

Make sure to dispose of your trash correctly, whether in a designated trash receptacle or carrying it home.

4. Observe Catch and Release Practices

If you're fishing for sport, consider practicing catch and release. This technique ensures that the fish population is not depleted and allows other fishermen to catch the same fish.

If you can observe all rules, regulations, and etiquette as we have discussed, you will not only have a stress-free time during fishing, but you'll also be doing right by the law, other fishermen, and the environment.

Conclusion

Hopefully, this book has taught you everything you need to begin your fishing adventure, from the right gear and tools to fishing techniques and boats.

You're now ready to go out there and have fun! All you need to do is follow the tips in this book, and you will have the most fantastic time of your life every time you are outdoors fishing.

Thanks so much for purchasing this book, I really hope you enjoyed it.

Please click the relevant link below to leave a review, it would be greatly appreciated!

US Customers Review

UK Customers Review

AUS Customers Review

Printed in Great Britain
by Amazon